D1644929

Cordon Bleu

Basic Cookery Methods

CBC / B.P.C. Publishing Ltd.

Published by
B.P.C. Publishing Ltd.,
St. Giles House, 49/50 Poland Street,
W1A 2LG

Copyright B.P.C. Publishing Ltd., 1972

Designed by Melvyn Kyte
Printed by Waterlow (Dunstable) Ltd.

These recipes have been adapted from the Cordon Bleu Cookery Course
published by Purnell in association with the London Cordon Bleu Cookery Schoo
Principal: Rosemary Hume. Co-principal: Muriel Downes

Quantities given are for 4 servings. Spoon measures are level unless otherwise
stated

Contents

Baking

How to make pastry

So many puddings are made with pastry that it is important to be able to make it well. Good pastry is not difficult if certain rules — which are often forgotten — are followed. The main points are:

1 Work in a cool, airy room. Plan to make the pastry before the kitchen becomes warm from other cooking because a damp, warm atmosphere is disastrous.

2 Use fresh, fine-sifted plain flour (self-raising flour or baking powder produces spongy-textured pastry), firm but not hard fat (which would not blend properly with the flour) and ice-cold water for mixing. Baking powder is sometimes used to lighten a rich pastry that has a lot of fat.

3 Handle flour and fat lightly but firmly. When rubbing fat into the flour, keep lifting it up and crumbling the mixture between your fingers. This movement helps to aerate the pastry. Shake the bowl after 1-2 minutes to bring the larger lumps of fat to the surface and to show you how much more rubbing-in is necessary. This is especially helpful when making rich shortcrust where over-rubbing makes the pastry greasy.

4 Make sure that the correct amount of water is added. This may vary a little with the quality of the flour. Too dry a mixture makes the pastry difficult to handle; it will crack when rolled out and crumble after baking and will be dry to eat. Too wet a dough will shrink and lose shape while baking, and also makes for tough, hard pastry. The amount of water is usually indicated in a recipe and it is important that at least two-thirds of the given quantity are added to the dry ingredients before mixing begins. This avoids over-working and brings the ingredients quickly to a firm, smooth pastry, especially when making the foundation dough for puff pastry.

5 A marble slab or slate shelf is ideal for rolling out pastry because it is smooth, solid and cool; otherwise, keep a board especially for this purpose (a laminated plastic surface is cool). Once pastry is rolled out, always scrape slab or board thoroughly before rolling out new pastry to remove any dough that may have stuck and which might cause further sticking. (This applies particularly to flaky or puff pastry when rolling out is of paramount importance.) Use a minimum amount of flour for dusting when rolling, otherwise too much will go into the pastry and spoil it. A heavy, plain wooden rolling pin without handles is best, especially for puff pastry.

6 Chill made pastry for about 30 minutes or leave it aside in a cool place for the same amount of time. This gives pastry a chance to relax and removes any elasticity which may cause shrinkage round edge of dish.

7 It is essential when baking pastry to pre-set the oven to the required temperature. The immediate heat sets the pastry in its correct shape and makes it possible to control the exact amount of cooking time.

Basic proportions

For shortcrust pastry the basic proportions of ingredients are half the amount of fat to the weight of flour, and $\frac{1}{4}$ oz salt to each lb flour. For rich shortcrust, allow 2 egg yolks to every lb flour. When more fat is added, as in many recipes using rich shortcrust, the pastry is shorter (ie. lighter and more crisp), and is best for pies and tarts to be eaten cold. Butter, margarine, lard or shortening (one of the commercially prepared cooking fats) may be used. A mixture of fats gives the best results, eg. butter and lard, as the former gives a good flavour and the latter a good texture.

When terms such as 8 oz pastry or an 8 oz quantity of pastry are used, this means the amount obtained by using 8 oz flour, not 8 oz prepared dough. As a guide, 8 oz shortcrust pastry will cover a 9-inch long pie dish holding $1\frac{1}{2}$ lb fruit, or line an 8-inch flan ring. For a covered plate pie (8-9 inches diameter), use 10 oz shortcrust pastry.

Shortcrust pastry

8 oz plain flour
pinch of salt
4–6 oz butter, margarine, lard or shortening (one of the commercially prepared fats), or a mixture of any two
3–4 tablespoons cold water

Method

Sift the flour with a pinch of salt into a mixing bowl. Cut the fat into the flour with a round-bladed knife and, as soon as the pieces are well coated with flour, rub in with the fingertips until the mixture looks like fine breadcrumbs.

Make a well in the centre, add the water (reserving about 1 tablespoon) and mix quickly with a knife. Press together with the fingers, adding the extra water, if necessary, to give a firm dough.

Turn on to a floured board, knead pastry lightly until smooth. Chill (wrapped in greaseproof paper, a polythene bag or foil) in refrigerator for 30 minutes before using.

Rich shortcrust pastry

8 oz plain flour
pinch of salt
6 oz butter
1 rounded dessertspoon caster sugar (for sweet pastry)
1 egg yolk
2–3 tablespoons cold water

Method

Sift the flour with a pinch of salt into a mixing bowl. Drop in the butter and cut it into the flour until the small pieces are well coated. Then rub them in with the fingertips until the mixture looks like fine breadcrumbs. Stir in the sugar, mix egg yolk with water, tip into the fat and flour and mix quickly with a palette knife to a firm dough.

Turn on to a floured board and knead lightly until smooth. If possible, chill (wrapped in greaseproof paper, a polythene bag or foil) in refrigerator for 30 minutes before using.

Pastry finishes

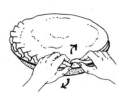

Crimp by pinching pastry edge between thumb and forefinger of each hand, twisting slightly in opposite directions.

Flute by pressing left thumb on top of outer edge. Draw back of knife towards centre for $\frac{1}{2}$ inch, repeating all way round. Leave $\frac{3}{4}$ inch between cuts for savoury pies, $\frac{1}{4}$ inch for sweet ones.

Flaky pastry

8 oz plain flour
pinch of salt
3 oz butter
3 oz lard
$\frac{1}{4}$ pint ice-cold water (to mix)

Method

Sift flour with salt into a bowl. Divide fats into four portions (two of butter, two of lard); rub one portion — either lard or butter — into flour and mix to a firm dough with cold water. The amount of water varies with different flour but an average quantity for 8 oz flour is 4-5 fluid oz (about $\frac{1}{4}$ pint or 8-10 tablespoons); the finer the flour the more water it will absorb.

Knead the dough lightly until smooth, then roll out to an oblong. Put a second portion of fat (not the same kind as first portion rubbed in) in small pieces on to two-thirds of the dough. Fold in three, half turn the dough to bring the open edge towards you and roll out again to an oblong. Put on a third portion of fat in pieces, fold dough in three, wrap in a cloth or polythene bag and leave in a cool place for 15 minutes.

Roll out again, put on rest of fat in pieces, fold and roll as before. If pastry looks streaky, turn once more and roll again.

1 *To make flaky pastry, mix fat and flour to a firm dough with a little ice-cold water*
2 *Knead dough, roll out to an oblong, dot second portion of fat over two-thirds of dough. Fold in three, half turn and roll out to an oblong. Repeat*
3 *Roll out the dough again, put on the last portion of fat and roll out as before*

Rough puff pastry 1

8 oz plain flour
pinch of salt
6 oz firm butter, or margarine
¼ pint ice-cold water (to mix)

The first of the two types of rough puff pastry is a quicker and less fussy one, although the same ingredients are used in both types. You can use either type in recipes but the second is likely to be a little lighter.

Method

Sift the flour with salt into a mixing bowl. Cut the fat in even-size pieces about the size of walnuts and drop into the flour. Mix quickly with the water (to prevent overworking dough so that it becomes starchy) and turn on to a lightly-floured board.

Complete the following action three times; roll to an oblong, fold in three and make a half-turn to bring the open edges in front of you so that the pastry has three turns in all. Chill for 10 minutes and give an extra roll and fold if it looks at all streaky, then use as required.

> Note: it is important to scrape off bits of dough left on pastry board, otherwise pastry made afterwards may pick it up and be lumpy.

Rough puff pastry 2

8 oz plain flour
pinch of salt
6 oz firm butter, or margarine
¼ pint ice-cold water (to mix)

Method

Sift the flour with salt into a mixing bowl. Take 1 oz of fat and rub it into the flour. Mix to a firm but pliable dough with the water, knead lightly until smooth, then set in a cool place for 10-15 minutes.

Place the remaining fat between two pieces of grease-proof paper and beat to a flat cake with the rolling pin. This fat should be the same consistency as the dough.

Roll out this dough to a rectangle, place the flattened fat in the middle, fold like a parcel and turn over.

Complete the following action three times: roll out dough to an oblong, fold in three and make a half-turn to bring the open edge towards you so that the pastry has three turns in all. Chill for 10 minutes, then roll out and use as required.

How to make puff pastry

Forming the dough

To have perfect results when making puff pastry, you must use the right kind of flour and fat, and always use ice-cold water for mixing.

It is also important to work in a very cool atmosphere. Never attempt to make puff pastry in very hot weather; it will become sticky and difficult to handle. Make it early in the morning (if possible before you have done any cooking), as a kitchen soon becomes warm and steamy.

Fat should be cool and firm. The best puff pastry for flavour and texture is made from butter; this should be of a firm consistency and slightly salted — such as English, Australian or New Zealand. Continental butters are too creamy in texture and result in a sticky pastry, difficult to handle.

If margarine has to be used, again use a firm variety (one that does not spread easily). The cheapest varieties of butter and margarine are the best for this purpose.

Flour should be 'strong', ie. a bread flour which has a high gluten content. It should also be well sifted and quite cool.

The flour is made into a firm dough with a little butter and the water. This preliminary mixing is most important as it is on this that the success of the pastry depends.

Add the lemon juice to approximately two-thirds of the given amount of water. Stir until a dough begins to form, then add remaining water. If water is added a little at a time, it will dry in the flour and the resulting dough will be tough. The finished dough should be firm yet pliable and have the consistency of butter, taking into account the different textures.

Knead the dough firmly — this and the presence of the lemon juice develops the gluten in the flour and means that the dough will stand the frequent rolling and folding necessary in the preparation of puff pastry.

The butter should be cool and firm, but not used straight from the refrigerator. If it is overhard (or not taken from the refrigerator early enough), put it between two pieces of damp greaseproof paper and beat it 2-3 times with the rolling pin. It is then ready to be rolled into the dough.

Rolling out the dough

The method of rolling is also important and differs slightly from the usual way. You roll shortcrust pastry to shape the dough; in puff pastry it is the rolling that actually makes it.

Always roll the dough away from you, keeping the pressure as even as possible. Many people are inclined to put more weight on the right or left hand, which pulls the dough to one side; keep it straight by applying even pressure all round.

Bring the rolling pin down smartly on to the dough and roll it forward with a strong, firm pressure in one direction only. Continue until just before the edge of the dough.

Watchpoint Never let the rolling pin run off the edge as the object is to keep the dough strictly rectangular in shape.

▶

How to make puff pastry continued

Lift the rolling pin and continue rolling forward in one direction, bringing it down at the point to which it was last rolled. In this way the whole area of the dough is rolled in even layers, $\frac{1}{2}$-$\frac{3}{4}$ inch thick.

Once rolled to an even rectangle, the dough is folded in three round the butter (see page 18). Graduate the thickness of the following rollings, so that these subsequent ones are progressively thinner. You must avoid pushing butter through the dough, which might happen if it were rolled thinly in the beginning.

Watchpoint Do not turn the dough over; it should only be rolled on one side.

Each rolling is called a 'turn'

and puff pastry usually has six turns with a 15-minute rest between every two. Before each turn the dough is folded in three (ends to middle) and the edges sealed with the side of the hand or the rolling pin to prevent the folds shifting when dough is rolled. The short period of rest is to remove any elasticity from the dough. If at the end of the rollings the dough is at all streaky (showing that the butter has not been rolled in completely), a seventh turn can be given.

Should fat begin to break through dough, stop at once. Dust dough with flour, brush off the surplus, and chill it for 10 minutes before continuing.

Once made, the pastry may be finally rolled out, cut to shape and stored, wrapped in grease-proof paper and a cloth. It need not be stored in a strip. It will keep for 24-48 hours in a cool place.

Save all trimmings and fold them in three. Place all trimmings on top of each other. Roll out and use for making jalousie and palmiers (see recipes given on page 26).

Baking pastry

If the uncooked pastry seems a little soft, place it on a baking sheet in refrigerator for about 15 minutes (no longer) for it to firm up before baking.

Place pastry on a thick baking sheet well dampened with cold water. This helps to prevent pastry from sliding and shrinking too much while baking. A thick baking sheet will not buckle in the hot oven.

Puff pastry is cooked in a hot oven at 425°F or Mark 7. A large case, such as a vol-au-vent or flan, is baked in the centre of the oven. Small pieces such as bouchées (miniature vol-au-vents) are baked on the top shelf about 5 inches from the roof of the oven. ▶

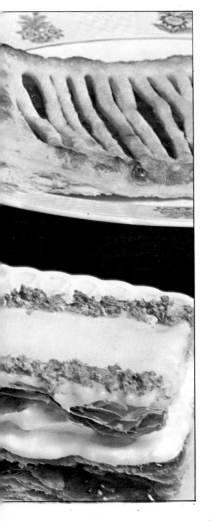

A whole mille feuilles (front), a fresh fruit flan and a jalousie   17

How to make puff pastry continued

Oven positions apply to gas ovens. Electric ovens vary according to where the elements are placed. Follow your electric cooker's instruction book.

1 *After first rolling out of the pastry, butter is laid on the centre and sides turned in over it*

2 *The pastry is folded into three, ends to middle, like a parcel*

3 *Rolling pin is brought down lightly on to the pastry to flatten it before rolling out*

4 *After each rolling, pastry is always folded into three, the ends pulled to keep them rectangular*

Basic puff pastry

8 oz plain flour
pinch of salt
8 oz butter
1 teaspoon lemon juice
scant $\frac{1}{4}$ pint water (ice-cold)

This quantity will make a vol-au-vent for 4 people or 6-8 $2\frac{1}{4}$-inch bouchées. Use up trimmings as recipes on page 26.

Method

Sift flour and salt into a bowl. Rub in a piece of butter the size of a walnut. Add lemon juice to water, make a well in centre of flour and pour in about two-thirds of the liquid. Mix with a palette, or round-bladed, knife. When the dough is beginning to form, add remaining water.

Turn out the dough on to a marble slab, a laminated plastic work top, or a board, dusted with flour. Knead dough for 2-3 minutes, then roll out to a square about $\frac{1}{2}$-$\frac{3}{4}$ inch thick.

Beat butter, if necessary, to make it pliable and place in centre of dough. Fold this up over butter to enclose it completely (sides and ends over centre like a parcel). Wrap in a cloth or piece of greaseproof paper and put in the refrigerator for 10-15 minutes.

Flour slab or work top, put on dough, the join facing upwards, and bring rolling pin down on to dough 3-4 times to flatten it slightly.

Now roll out to a rectangle about $\frac{1}{2}$-$\frac{3}{4}$ inch thick. Fold into three, ends to middle, as accurately as possible, if necessary pulling the ends to keep them rectangular. Seal the edges with your hand or rolling pin and turn pastry half round to bring the edge towards you. Roll out again and fold in three (keep a note of the 'turns' given). Set pastry aside in refrigerator for 15 minutes.

Repeat this process, giving a total of 6 turns with three 15-minute rests after each two turns. Then leave in the refrigerator until wanted.

> **Note:** it is important to scrape off bits of dough left on the pastry board, otherwise pastry made afterwards may pick them up and be lumpy.

> **A bouchée** (mouthful) is similar to a vol-au-vent but smaller. Individual bouchées served as an entrée are about $2\frac{1}{4}$ inches in diameter, and for cocktail savouries 1–$1\frac{1}{2}$ inches in diameter. The fillings are savoury and can be the same as for vol-au-vents.

How to make choux pastry

Although a quick and easy pastry to make, choux does call for care in measuring ingredients, otherwise results may be uneven and unsuccessful. You will find that it is better to weigh dry ingredients on scales rather than use a tablespoon for measuring them.

General points

Choux pastry is not made like other types of pastry. The fat is put into a pan with water and, when this has boiled, the flour is poured in and beaten. It is important, however, that you only beat the flour until the pastry is smooth; this takes a few seconds only. Continued beating at this stage will mean that the pastry will not rise.

Use plain flour, or, for a particularly crisp result, a 'strong' flour (one with a good gluten content). This type of flour is now available in good stores throughout the country.

Once the eggs have been added, the pastry should then be beaten thoroughly. An electric mixer can be used at this stage with the paddle or dough hook on slow speed.

Choux pastry should be baked in a hot oven on a rising temperature, ie. cooked for 10 minutes at 400°F or Mark 6, then the cooking completed at 425°F or Mark 7 for the length of time given in the recipe. This will ensure that the choux is brown and crisp. If it is still pale in colour, it will collapse when taken out of the oven.

Choux is usually baked on a dampened baking sheet (hold sheet under the cold tap for a few seconds). Once baked and taken off the sheet to cool, make a hole in the side of the choux pastry with a skewer or the point of knife to release any steam and so keep it crisp.

Once baked choux pastry does not keep well and should be used within 2-3 hours.

Basic choux pastry

Quantity for 3–4 people
$\frac{1}{4}$ pint (5 fl oz) water
2 oz butter, or margarine
$2\frac{1}{2}$ oz plain flour
2 eggs

Quantity for 4–6 people
$7\frac{1}{2}$ fl oz water
3 oz butter, or margarine
$3\frac{3}{4}$ oz plain flour
3 eggs

Method

Put water and fat into a fairly large pan. Sift flour on to a piece of paper. Bring contents of the pan to the boil and when bubbling draw pan aside, allow bubbles to subside and pour in all the flour at once. Stir vigorously until it is smooth (a few seconds).

Cool mixture for about 5 minutes, then beat in the eggs one at a time. If eggs are large, break the last one into a bowl and beat with a fork. Add this slowly to ensure that the mixture remains firm and keeps its shape (you may not need to use all of this last egg).

Beat pastry for about 3 minutes until it looks glossy. It is then ready to be used according to the recipe.

American pie pastry

Pastry for the American covered pie is slightly different from shortcrust both in ingredients and method. Most recipes for American shortcrust have a high proportion of fat to flour, and usually need more liquid for binding. This is because American and Canadian flour is milled from hard wheat which is very high in gluten (the major part of the protein content of wheat flour, which gives it its elasticity), and consequently absorbs more liquid.

The following recipe is an anglicised version, but has the same short, melt-in-the-mouth texture. As the texture is very short, the pastry is not easy to handle once cooked, so serve the pie in the dish in which it is baked (a round, shallow tin or dish—pie plate—about 2-2½ inches deep). The pastry is lined into the pie plate, fruit placed on top, and the pie is then covered with a lid of pastry.

Basic recipe

5 oz lard, or shortening
pinch of salt
2 tablespoons cold water
8 oz self-raising flour

Method

Place the lard or shortening in a bowl, add a good pinch of salt and the water, and cream ingredients together. Sift the flour over the softened fat and, using a round-bladed knife, cut the fat into the flour and mix to a rough dough. Chill for 30 minutes.

Turn the dough on to a floured board, knead lightly and then use for covered fruit pies.

Yorkshire apple cake (a plate pie)

For shortcrust pastry
6 oz plain flour
pinch of salt
2½ oz butter
1½ oz lard, or shortening
2 tablespoons cold water

For filling
1½ lb cooking apples
½ oz butter
1 strip of peel and juice of ½ lemon
2 tablespoons thick honey or
   3–4 tablespoons sugar

8-inch diameter ovenproof plate or dish

Method

Make the shortcrust pastry (see page 12) and set aside to chill.

Butter a shallow pan. Peel core and slice (not too thinly) apples, put into the pan with all other ingredients. Cover and cook gently until juice begins to run, then remove lid and cook quickly to a thick pulp, stirring frequently. Turn out on to a plate to cool.

Roll out a little less than half of the pastry to a round and line on to the ovenproof plate or dish, pressing down and trimming off the edge. Turn the apple mixture on to this plate or dish, flatten and brush the edge with water. Roll out the rest of the pastry, keeping it thicker than the bottom piece, and lay this over the plate or dish. Press and crimp round edge (see page 12). Leave plain or dry glaze (brush pastry lightly with water and dust with caster sugar). Stand plate or dish on a baking sheet and bake for 35-45 minutes in an oven pre-set at 375 °F or Mark 5.

Bakewell tart

6 oz rich shortcrust pastry

For filling
1 tablespoon strawberry jam
1 tablespoon lemon curd
1 oz butter
2 oz caster sugar
grated rind and juice of ½ lemon
1 egg
2 oz ground almonds
2 rounded tablespoons sponge cake
   crumbs

7-inch diameter sandwich tin

Method

Set the pastry aside to chill. When chilled, roll it out and line on to the sandwich tin. Spread the pastry first with jam and then with lemon curd.

Cream the butter in a bowl until soft, add the sugar and lemon rind and continue beating until light. Beat egg, add a little at a time, and then stir in the almonds, cake crumbs and lemon juice. Spread the almond mixture over the lemon curd and bake for 35–45 minutes until set and golden-brown in an oven pre-set at 375 °F or Mark 5.

Eccles cakes

8 oz flaky pastry (well chilled)

For filling
1 oz butter
1 rounded tablespoon soft brown sugar
4 oz currants
little grated nutmeg, or mixed spice
1 rounded tablespoon finely chopped candied peel
1 egg white (beaten)
caster sugar

Method

Set oven at 425°F or Mark 7.

Melt the butter and stir in the sugar; add the currants, well washed and still wet, the nutmeg, or spice, and finely chopped peel.

Roll out the pastry very thinly, turn over and cut into 6-inch diameter rounds (use a saucer to cut round). Put a good tablespoon of filling in the centre of each round and damp pastry edges, draw to the centre and pinch well together. Turn pastry over, flatten gently with the rolling pin so the currants just show through, but still keep the cakes round. Make three small cuts on the top, brush with egg white, dust with caster sugar, place on a baking sheet and bake in preset oven for 10-15 minutes, or until golden.

Cream horns

8 oz rough puff pastry (well chilled)
1 egg white (beaten)
strawberry, or raspberry, jam
$\frac{1}{4}$ pint Chantilly cream
pistachio nuts (finely chopped)
— for decoration

12 cream horn moulds

Method

Lightly grease the moulds and a baking sheet. Set the oven at 425°F or Mark 7.

Roll out the pastry $\frac{1}{8}$-inch thick, cut into long, 1-inch wide strips and brush these with a very little beaten egg white. Wind the pastry round the cream horn moulds, starting at the point and overlapping each round. Trim the tops, brush again with egg white, set on a lightly greased baking sheet and bake for 7-8 minutes until crisp and pale golden-brown.

Remove the horns from the tins. When cold, put a $\frac{1}{2}$ teaspoon of jam at the bottom of each horn and fill with Chantilly cream. Decorate the top of each one with a small pinch of pistachio nuts.

Chantilly cream

Whip a $\frac{1}{4}$-pint carton of double cream until just thickening; then add 1 teaspoon caster sugar and 2-3 drops of vanilla essence. Then continue beating until the cream holds its shape. (In warm weather and in a warm kitchen, if the sugar and essence are added before first whisking, it prevents cream getting thick.)

Steak and kidney pie

1½ lb skirt, or sticking, of beef
6 oz ox kidney
salt and pepper
1 tablespoon flour
1 shallot, or ½ small onion (finely chopped)
1 teaspoon chopped parsley (optional)
½ pint cold water, or stock
hot water, or stock (to dilute gravy)
egg wash

For flaky pastry

8 oz flour
3 oz lard
3 oz butter
about 8 tablespoons cold water

10-inch pie dish, pie funnel

Method

Prepare the flaky pastry (see page 13). Well grease the pie dish. Set oven at 425°F or Mark 7.

Cut the beef into 1-inch cubes; skin and core kidney and cut into pieces; roll both well in seasoned flour (for this amount of meat add as much salt as you can hold between two fingers and your thumb, and half as much pepper, to the 1 tablespoon of flour).

Place meat in the pie dish, sprinkling each layer with the shallot and parsley, and set the pie funnel in the centre. Pour in the cold water or stock and cover pie with the pastry in the following way.

Roll out prepared pastry ¼-inch thick and cut off a piece large enough to cover and over-lap the top of the pie dish; roll the remainder a little thinner and cut two strips, each ½ inch wide. Damp the edge of the pie dish, press on the strips of pastry and brush with water. Lift the sheet of pastry on your rolling pin and cover the prepared pie.

Watchpoint Do not stretch pastry when covering pie or it will shrink during cooking and slide into the pie dish. When trimming the pastry to fit the dish, lift the pie on one hand and, holding a knife at an angle away from the dish, cut the overlapping pastry in short brisk strokes. To trim in one continuous cut would drag the pastry, spoil the appearance and prevent it rising in good flakes.

Seal the edges of the double thickness of pastry. Flute the edge (see page 12). Any remaining strips or trimmings of pastry can be used to cut a centre decoration of a rose or thistle, and leaves.

Brush egg wash over top of pie. Arrange the centre decoration and brush with egg wash.

Bake 20-30 minutes in the pre-set oven, then cover the pie with a large sheet of damp greaseproof paper, pleating and twisting it under the dish to hold it in place. This prevents the pastry getting too brown and hard during the long cooking which follows. Reduce the oven heat to 325°F or Mark 3 and cook for a further 1½ hours.

To serve: as the gravy in the pie is very strong and con-centrated, have ready a small jug of hot stock or water and, when the first portion of pastry is cut, pour in a little to dilute and increase the quantity of gravy for serving.

Lining a flan case

8 oz puff pastry
egg wash

Two pan lids, or rings (8-inch and 6-inch diameters)

Method

Set oven at 425°F or Mark 7.

Roll out puff pastry, a scant ½-inch thick.

To cut flan case: cut out a round with larger lid, keeping a straight edge. With smaller lid cut out a centre circle (see photograph, right). You will then have one outer ring (1 inch wide) and one large round (6 inches in diameter).

Slide this outer ring to one side and re-roll 6-inch round with any trimmings to make a larger but thinner round (about ¼-inch thick and 8 inches in diameter) to form flan base.

Lift this round of pastry on to the damp baking sheet, brush very lightly with egg wash, then lift the ring on to it. Neaten both layers into a perfect round and cut away any surplus pastry. Brush top of the ring with egg wash and mark with the back of a knife in diagonal lines to decorate.

Prick the centre with a fork, chill 10-15 minutes in refrigerator, then bake in pre-set oven for 25-30 minutes. Cool slightly before sliding off baking sheet. The flan case is now ready for a savoury or sweet filling.

To make a flan case, first cut out a large round, then cut a smaller centre circle from it, using a smaller pan lid. Re-roll this smaller circle with the trimmings and make a larger but thinner one to form flan base. The outer ring is then lifted on to it

An egg wash is made by beating 1 egg with ½ teaspoon of salt. This liquefies the egg, which makes it easier to brush a thin film on pastry, and also increases the shine when baked.

Palmiers

6 oz puff pastry, or trimmings
caster sugar

Method

Roll out pastry to a strip. Dredge well with caster sugar, fold in three and roll out again. Dust once more with sugar, fold in three and roll out. Fold in three again and chill for 15 minutes.

Set oven at 425°F or Mark 7. Roll out pastry to a 10-inch square, about a $\frac{1}{4}$-inch thick. Fold the edge nearest to you twice over to reach the centre of pastry; repeat this from the other side. Press lightly with rolling pin, then fold in half.

Press again, then with a sharp knife cut across into slices about $\frac{1}{2}$-inch wide. Lay these, cut side down, on a dampened baking sheet, leaving room for them to spread. Open slices slightly, and flatten with the heel of the hand. Bake in pre-set oven for 10-12 minutes. (See shape below.)

When beginning to go brown, turn them over so that both sides will caramelise. When brown and sticky lift off on to a rack to cool. Serve plain or sandwiched with cream.

Jalousie

6 oz puff pastry, or trimmings
4 tablespoons jam (gooseberry, apricot or plum)
1 egg white
caster sugar (for dusting)

Method

Set oven at 425°F or Mark 7.

Roll out pastry to a large rectangle, $\frac{1}{4}$-inch thick. Trim and cut out a piece approximately 8 inches by 4 inches. Fold this piece over lengthways and, with a sharp knife, cut across fold at $\frac{1}{4}$-inch intervals, but not right to outer edges, leaving a border of about 1-1$\frac{1}{2}$ inches.

Fold up trimmings and roll out thinly to a rectangle twice the size of folded pastry; lift on to dampened baking sheet.

Spoon the jam down the centre, spreading it out a little. Brush the edges with cold water, then lift the first on to the second rectangle of pastry, with the folded edge on the centre. Open out the folded pastry and press the border down on to the lower piece. Cut round edges to neaten, chill for 10 minutes, if necessary, then bake in pre-set oven for 25-30 minutes.

From 5-10 minutes before it's cooked take out of the oven and brush with egg white, beaten to a froth, and dust well with caster sugar. Replace in the oven and remove jalousie when a golden-brown.

Slide on to a rack to cool. Serve hot or cold.

Vol-au-vent

8 oz puff pastry (well chilled)
egg wash

Pan lid (6-7 inch diameter), 3-4 inch
diameter plain cutter

Method

Set oven at 425°F or Mark 7.

Roll out the puff pastry on a floured slab or work top to a square, $\frac{1}{2}$-$\frac{3}{4}$ inches thick.

To cut vol-au-vent shape: place pan lid on pastry and cut round it with a knife; hold the knife slantwise to form a bevelled edge, wider at the base. Turn the round upside down on to a dampened baking sheet, so that the widest part is on top. Brush lightly with the egg wash.

Watchpoint Egg wash acts as a seal, so don't let it touch the cut edge or it will stop the pastry from rising.

With the cutter (or a small pan lid), mark a circle in the centre of round with the back of a knife and mark lines for decoration. Chill pastry 10-15 minutes if it seems a little soft, then bake in pre-set oven for 25-30 minutes.

When well risen and a good colour, slide on to a rack to cool. While still warm cut round the circular mark with the point of a small knife to remove the top. Set this aside and carefully scoop out some of the soft centre. Place vol-au-vent case on serving dish before filling. (It can be baked beforehand but do not add filling until just before serving.)

Vol-au-vents can be filled with shellfish, veal, chicken, sweetbreads and mushrooms, bound with a white or velouté sauce.

1 *Make a vol-au-vent shape by placing a pan lid on the rolled out pastry and cutting round it*

2 *Place pastry underside up on baking sheet; mark out centre circle and lines for decoration*

3 *When cooked, cut out the centre circle and scoop out some of soft vol-au-vent centre. The case is then ready for filling*

English cakes

There are a great variety of ways to make English cakes, but whichever recipe you choose, one of the most important aspects is the initial preparation. The success and impact of a home-baked cake in flavour, texture and appearance hinge on this factor. Flavour and texture are dependent on the choice and preparation of the right ingredients. Don't gaily substitute plain for self-raising flour and then complain when you get a sad cake, and do mix ingredients thoroughly in the early stages.

Appearance depends largely on neat and expert preparation of the cake tin. Cut lining paper to fit exactly; if it has lumps and bumps the finished cake will be bumpy to match.

Preparation of ingredients

Flour should always be sifted with a good pinch of salt before use. Sifting aerates the flour and removes any small lumps; the salt improves the flavour.

Keep both plain and self-raising flour in your cupboard so that you can use whichever is indicated in a recipe.

Fats play a large part in the success of each cake, and different kinds are suitable for different recipes. Butter is the perfect fat for cake-making because it gives a wonderful flavour and improves the keeping properties of the cake. Margarine, which is easier to cream, can be used in place of butter in nearly every recipe.

Shortening, or a cooking compound, gives very good results, particularly where the proportion of sugar and liquid in the recipe is high. These lard or vegetable fats contain no curd, and if stored properly will keep for many months.

A good beef dripping gives excellent results for plain luncheon cakes, but before use it must be clarified in the following way: turn the dripping into a bowl and pour on an equal amount of boiling water. Stir well, then leave it to set. Remove the solidified fat, scrape away any impurities from the underneath and then heat it gently until it no longer bubbles. Pour into an enamel basin and leave to set.

Sugars are very important. Using the wrong type will completely spoil a cake. Fine caster sugar must be used for all creamed cake mixtures. A coarse sugar results in cakes with spotted tops. Granulated sugar can be used for all mixtures which are 'rubbed in.' Demerara sugar should only be used in recipes where the sugar is dissolved and added to the cake mixture in liquid form, eg. gingerbread made by using the 'warming' method.

Soft brown sugar is good for luncheon and fruit cakes. Barbados sugar (dark brown, rich and moist) is used for rich fruit, wedding, birthday and Christmas cakes to improve the flavour. Some recipes may replace Barbados sugar with caster sugar and black treacle mixed together.

English cakes continued

Eggs are essential to make cakes light. They expand and coagulate on heating and so trap any air which is beaten into the mixture.

Fruit, nuts and candied peel. All dried fruit, unless clearly marked as washed and ready for use, should be cleaned. Gritty fruit can spoil the texture and the flavour of the cake.

When using nuts, check the recipe to see whether they should be shredded, flaked or chopped. This seemingly small variation has a decided effect on flavour, texture and appearance, particularly when the nuts are used to finish the cake.

Choose candied peel in caps; as a rule it is softer and fuller in flavour than the chopped variety. Scoop out the sugar from the centre and then shred the peel on a grater. This way you obtain the very best flavour and the fine slivers look attractive in the finished cake.

Raising agents. Baking powder is a commercial preparation made up of two parts cream of tartar and one part bicarbonate of soda. It should be sifted with plain flour in the proportion given in the recipe.

Bicarbonate of soda can be used instead, combined with soured milk, buttermilk, vinegar or black treacle. The proportions to replace 2 teaspoons of baking powder are $\frac{1}{2}$ teaspoon bicarbonate of soda to $\frac{1}{3}$ pint soured milk or buttermilk. This is only suitable for scones or very plain cake mixtures as the proportion of liquid is so high.

Use $\frac{1}{2}$ teaspoon bicarbonate of soda plus 1 tablespoon vinegar or black treacle for everyday fruit cakes.

Sifting 8 oz plain flour with 2 level teaspoons of baking powder gives the same result as using self-raising flour.

Ways of mixing

Rubbing-in method. This is used for small cakes and luncheon cakes. These are always meant to be eaten fresh, or at least within 2-3 days of baking. The fat is cut in small pieces, added to sifted flour, then rubbed lightly with the fingertips until it resembles fine breadcrumbs.

Warming (or boiled) method. This is suited to gingerbread, and some fruit cakes. A variety of raising agents is used with this method and as a general rule the texture is damp and close and so will improve with keeping.

Fat, sugar and liquids are melted in a saucepan before being added to flour. The mixture before baking (called cake batter) is much thinner than ordinary mixtures and is easily poured into prepared tin.

Creaming method. This is suited to all rich cakes and gives a light, even-textured cake with a soft, slightly moist top which should be smooth and perfectly flat.

For the very best results, follow these rules. First have the butter or margarine and eggs at room temperature (about 70°F). At this temperature the mixture is easier to beat and is less likely to curdle.

Beat the sugar a little at a time into the well-creamed butter, scraping the sides of the bowl once or twice during this process. If you leave any sugar crystals on the sides of the bowl, this will give the finished cake a speckled top.

When the butter and sugar look like whipped cream the eggs may be added. If the amount of sugar is **under** 8 oz, the eggs should be whisked together and added a little at a time. If using **more than** 8 oz sugar, the eggs may be added one at a time. After each addition of egg the mixture must be well beaten.

Watchpoint It is at this stage that curdling is most likely to happen. It is caused either because the butter and sugar have not been thoroughly creamed, or because the eggs are very cold. This curdling can be corrected by standing the mixing bowl in a little hot water and beating vigorously. If, however, you still have more egg to add, stir in 1 tablespoon of the sifted flour with each further addition of egg.

Then, using a metal spoon, gently fold in the flour and any liquid given in the recipe. Do not beat or stir; this will remove air beaten in and make the cake rise and crack.

Baking

First prepare the cake tins (see right), then turn on the oven, set the temperature and arrange the shelves before mixing the cake. There must be room for the heat to circulate in the oven round baking sheets and cake tins, otherwise the underneath of the cakes will burn.

If you are baking more than one cake in an oven that has back burners or elements, arrange the cakes side by side. If you have an oven with side burners, arrange the cakes back and front. A centre shelf is the best position for baking a cake.

Do not move the cake until the mixture is set and avoid opening the oven door until the minimum time given in the recipe is reached. This is a guide to cooking time but you should always test a cake before removing it from the oven. Creamed cake mixtures should spring back when pressed lightly with the finger-tips. Fruit cakes are tested by piercing with a trussing needle or fine skewer which should come away clean.

Preparation of tins

Brush sides and base of shallow tins with melted fat, line base with circle of buttered grease-proof paper and dust with flour. With tins over 2 inches in depth, sides should also be lined with buttered greaseproof paper which should be deep enough to stand 1 inch above the rim of the tin.

Victoria sandwich

about 6 oz butter
about 6 oz caster sugar
3 large eggs
about 6 oz self-raising flour
pinch of salt
1–2 tablespoons milk

To finish
3 tablespoons warm jam, or
   lemon curd
caster sugar (for dredging)

Deep 8-inch diameter sandwich tin

To make a good Victoria sandwich, weigh eggs in their shells and use exact equivalent of butter, sugar and flour.

Method

Grease and line sandwich tin; set the oven at 350°F or Mark 4.

Using the creaming method, soften the butter in a bowl, add the sugar and cream them together until soft and light. Whisk the eggs, add a little at a time and then beat thoroughly. Sift the flour with the salt and fold into the mixture a third at a time, adding enough milk to make the mixture drop easily from the spoon. Spread the mixture in the prepared tin and bake in pre-set oven for about 40-45 minutes.

To test if cake is ready press lightly with fingertips and it should spring back. The colour should be golden-brown, and the cake shrunk from sides of the tin. Have two wire cooling racks ready, and put a folded clean tea towel or double thickness of absorbent paper on one of them. Loosen the sides of the cake with a round-bladed knife, place the rack with the towel or paper on top of the cake (towel next to it) and turn over; remove the tin and disc of paper from the base. Place second rack on top of cake base and carefully and quickly turn it over again. This prevents the cake having the marks of cake rack on its top.

When the cake is cool split in half, fill with jam or lemon curd; dust top with caster sugar.

Madeira cake

8 oz butter
grated rind of ½ lemon
10 oz caster sugar
5 eggs
13 oz plain flour
pinch of salt
1 rounded teaspoon baking
   powder
1 teacup milk
slice of candied citron peel

8-inch diameter cake tin

Method

Prepare the cake tin and set the oven at 350°F or Mark 4.

Cream the butter with the grated lemon rind in a bowl, add the sugar gradually and continue beating until the mixture is light and soft. Beat in the eggs one at a time, each with 1 dessertspoon of flour, and then sift the remaining flour with the salt and baking powder and fold into the mixture with the milk. Turn into the prepared tin and bake in pre-set oven for about 1½ hours.

After the first 30 minutes place the slice of citron peel on top of the cake, and after 1 hour reduce the heat to 325°F or Mark 3. Test as for Victoria sandwich.

Gingerbread

4 oz butter
8 oz golden syrup
3 oz granulated sugar
1 tablespoon orange marmalade
¼ pint milk
4 oz self-raising flour
pinch of salt
1 teaspoon ground ginger
1 teaspoon mixed spice
½ teaspoon bicarbonate of soda
4 oz wholemeal flour
2 small eggs (well beaten)

8-inch square cake tin

Method

Prepare tin and set the oven at 325°F or Mark 3.

Heat the butter, syrup, sugar, marmalade and milk together in a saucepan and stir gently until the sugar dissolves. Allow the mixture to cool a little. Meanwhile sift the self-raising flour with the salt, spices and soda into a mixing bowl, add the wholemeal flour and then mix together.

Add the butter and syrup mixture to the beaten eggs and then pour into the dry ingredients. Stir with a wooden spoon until a smooth batter is formed, then pour into the prepared tin and bake in pre-set oven for about 1½ hours. Gingerbread is ready when pressed with fingertips and it springs back into place.

This gingerbread has a nice spongy texture and is cut into squares for serving.

Raisin dripping cake

1 lb plain flour
$\frac{1}{2}$ teaspoon salt
6 oz dripping
8 oz raisins
2 oz candied peel
6 oz granulated sugar
1 tablespoon black treacle
about $\frac{1}{4}$ pint milk
2 eggs (beaten)
1 teaspoon bicarbonate of soda

8-inch square cake tin

Method

Prepare cake tin and set oven at 350°F or Mark 4.

Sift the flour with the salt into a bowl and rub in the dripping thoroughly.

Remove stones from raisins, shred the candied peel and add these to the flour with the sugar.

Warm the treacle in a quarter of the milk, mix this with the beaten eggs and stir into the cake mixture with enough cold milk to make a dough of dropping consistency, ie. that will just drop from the wooden spoon when shaken.

Next add the bicarbonate of soda (dissolved in 1 tablespoon milk). Put mixture into the prepared tin immediately and bake in pre-set oven for $1\frac{1}{2}$-2 hours, reducing the temperature to 325°F or Mark 3 after the first hour. Cake is ready when a fine skewer comes away cleanly.

This cake is good thinly sliced or cut into squares and buttered.

Walnut bread

4 oz granulated sugar
6 oz golden syrup
small teacup milk (scant $\frac{1}{3}$ pint)
2 oz sultanas
8 oz flour
pinch of salt
3 teaspoons baking powder
2 oz walnuts (roughly chopped)
1 egg (beaten)

Loaf tin, $8\frac{1}{2}$ inches by $4\frac{1}{2}$ inches by $2\frac{1}{2}$ inches deep

Method

Grease and flour loaf tin. Set oven at 350 °F or Mark 4.

Heat the sugar, syrup, milk and sultanas in a saucepan and stir gently until the sugar is dissolved; allow to cool.

Sift the flour, salt and baking powder into bowl and add the roughly chopped walnuts. Tip the sugar and syrup mixture on to the beaten egg and then pour into the middle of the dry ingredients. Stir until smooth. Pour into the prepared tin and bake in pre-set oven for about $1\frac{1}{2}$ hours. Test as for Victoria sandwich.

Boiling and steaming

Boiling

Boiling is the most simple and economical form of cooking. The word implies that the food is immersed and cooked in water and for better or worse has become known internationally as the English way of cooking. (You will always find plainly boiled potatoes described on a continental menu as Pommes à l'anglaise.) 'Boiled' custard or fish, however, are inaccurately named as neither is boiled; both must be cooked well under boiling point.

Meat can be boiled in two different ways:

1 A joint such as leg of mutton is plunged into boiling salted water and boiled for 5 minutes to firm the outside and so seal in the juices. The heat is then reduced and the meat simmered until tender. Place the meat in the pan with the side that is to be uppermost when dished up on the bottom. Skim frequently during cooking time and allow 20-25 minutes per pound and 20-25 minutes over.

2 Meat for soups, stocks and beef tea is covered with cold water, salt added, and then allowed to stand for up to 20 minutes before cooking. This is because cold water and salt draw out the juices of the meat. Length of cooking time depends on the weight of meat and only gentle heat should be applied. To get as much flavour into liquid as possible, cut meat into small pieces.

Note: salted meats — beef, ham, pork and tongue should be put into tepid water to prevent over-saltiness.

Boiled chicken with parsley sauce

1 large boiling fowl, or roasting chicken
1 large carrot (quartered)
1 large onion (quartered)
bouquet garni
6 peppercorns
½ teaspoon salt
cold water
streaky bacon rashers

For parsley sauce
2 large handfuls of fresh parsley
¾ pint milk
1 bayleaf
1 blade of mace
6 peppercorns
1½ oz butter
2 rounded tablespoons flour
salt and pepper

This recipe is a typical example of the first method of boiling.

Method

Set the bird on its back in a large saucepan. Surround with the quartered vegetables, add the bouquet garni, peppercorns and salt. For a boiling fowl pour in enough water barely to cover; for a roasting chicken, sufficient just to cover the thighs. Cover saucepan and bring slowly to the boil. Simmer boiling fowl for 2-3 hours until tender; roasting fowl for 50-60 minutes. Turn bird over from time to time. When cooked draw saucepan aside and cool.

To prepare the sauce: pick parsley sprigs from stalks and wash well; reserve some stalks. Boil sprigs for 7 minutes in a saucepan of salted water, drain, press and rub through a bowl strainer to make about 1 dessertspoon of parsley purée.

Meanwhile infuse the milk with the bayleaf, mace, peppercorns, reserved parsley stalks. Strain. Melt the butter, stir in flour, blend in milk and stir until boiling. Season, simmer for 2-3 minutes, add parsley purée.

Remove rind from the bacon, and cut rashers in half. Grill or dry fry and keep hot. Take up chicken, remove the skin if using a boiling fowl.

Carve the bird and dish up. Coat with parsley sauce, garnish with bacon, and serve separately any remaining sauce. Serve boiled rice or creamed potato with this dish.

Steaming

Steaming is cooking by moist heat, a comparatively slow method as the food does not come into direct contact with boiling water but only with its vapour. Steaming food takes half as long again as boiling, and twice as long if the texture of the food is particularly dense.

There are two ways of steaming:
1 Using a steamer — a container with perforations at the bottom and a close-fitting lid. This can be bought with graduated ridges at the base rim so that it will fit snugly on to saucepans of varying sizes. For a perfect fit, saucepans can be bought complete with matching steamers. The food is placed directly in the top half — the steamer — and therefore comes in immediate contact with the steam. This method is used for vegetables such as potatoes, puddings, fish and poultry. Different foods wrapped separately in parchment paper can be cooked together in one steamer.
2 Using two plates. The food to be cooked is put between two plates over a pan of boiling water and cooks in its own juice and steam. The result is delicate in flavour and easily digested — an ideal way of cooking for invalids.

Two methods of steaming. Left, steaming chops between two plates over a saucepan of boiling water makes the meat more easily digested. Right, using a saucepan with a matching steamer for vegetables, puddings, fish or poultry

How to make suet and sponge puddings

Suet puddings should be rich yet light and to get this result, use breadcrumbs to lighten the flour and butcher's suet for flavour (chop finely — membranes are then more easily removed — and dust with flour to prevent sticking).

If you like to ring the changes in your menu, the following basic proportions will be useful. At any time up to half the flour can be replaced with the same weight of fresh breadcrumbs.

Basic recipe

8 oz plain flour
3–5 oz butcher's suet
$\frac{1}{2}$ teaspoon salt
2 teaspoons baking powder, or $\frac{1}{2}$ teaspoon bicarbonate of soda if treacle is used in recipe and you like a dark pudding
1–4 oz sugar
1–4 tablespoons treacle, golden syrup, marmalade or jam, or
2–6 oz dried fruit
1 egg
sufficient milk (about $\frac{1}{4}$ pint if no other liquid is used) to give a dropping consistency, ie. that will just drop from a wooden spoon when shaken

Method

Well grease a pudding basin and have ready a saucepan of boiling water. (If boiling the pudding, there should be enough water to cover the basin completely; if steaming without a steamer, the water should not come more than half-way up basin.)

Sieve the flour with the salt and baking powder (or bicarbonate of soda) into a mixing bowl. If using fresh butcher's suet, remove skin, shred and chop finely, removing membranes. (Use a little of the measured flour to prevent suet sticking.) Add the remaining ingredients to the flour, using enough milk to give a dropping consistency.

Mix well and turn at once into the prepared basin. Cover with pieces of well-buttered greaseproof paper and foil, both with two 1-inch pleats in the centre, at right-angles to each other, to allow the pudding to rise. Tie down with string. Or for boiling, cover with a scalded cloth, floured on the underside and pleated in the centre.

Tie the cloth round basin rim and knot the four corners back over the top. Make a loop of string after tying to prevent burnt hands when removing basin from the steamer.

Boil for $2\frac{1}{2}$ hours, or steam for 3 hours, ensuring that the water is kept boiling all the time and topped up regularly with boiling water.

39

Marguerite pudding

5 oz self-raising flour
pinch of salt
2½ oz butter
2½ oz caster sugar
1 large egg
6–7 tablespoons milk
3 tablespoons raspberry, or plum jam

For sauce
extra jam
little lemon juice and water, mixed

Method

Grease basin and have ready a saucepan half full of boiling water.

Sieve flour with salt into a bowl, rub in butter, then add sugar. Whisk egg with half of the milk and stir into mixture. Add remaining milk, if necessary, to give a dropping consistency.

Spoon jam into basin, fill with mixture on top. Cover with greaseproof paper and foil (make 1-inch pleats to allow pudding to rise), tie securely round basin with string, leaving a long loop to facilitate lifting out basin, steam for 1½–2 hours. Turn on to a hot dish, serve with a sauce made from extra jam heated and thinned with a little water and lemon juice.

Note: this pudding can be made with golden syrup or marmalade and served with a matching sauce made as above.

Spotted dick

8 oz self-raising flour
pinch of salt
4 oz butter
2 rounded tablespoons caster sugar
6 oz currants (washed)
2 eggs
little milk

Method

Sift the flour with the salt into a basin, rub in butter and then stir in the sugar and currants. Whisk the eggs, add to the mixture and stir until smooth with a wooden spoon, adding milk, if necessary, to give a dropping consistency.

Turn into a well-greased basin, cover as before, tie securely and steam for 1½–2 hours. Serve with custard.

The steamed puddings above, a little lighter in texture than a suet pudding, are made by the same method as plain cake mixtures. Here the fat is rubbed into the flour and each recipe mentions butter which does, of course, give an excellent flavour, but in every case this can be replaced by margarine or a commercially prepared shortening.

Vegetables

Many people do not realise that quite ordinary vegetables can be turned into excellent lunch or supper dishes. With a cheese or béchamel sauce your vegetable is transformed into an attractive and substantial main dish.

Vegetables

A selection of colourful vegetables

Stuffed mushrooms

2 mushrooms per person, and 2–3
    extra
$\frac{1}{2}$ oz butter
1 teaspoon chopped onion
1 tablespoon fresh white bread-
    crumbs, or slice of crust soaked
    in milk
salt and pepper
1 teaspoon parsley
pinch of dried mixed herbs

Method

Cup mushrooms are best for
this dish. Wash and peel them,
then cut across the stalks level
with the caps. Chop the trimmings with extra mushrooms.
Cook 1–2 minutes in the butter
with chopped onion. Add
crumbs (or soaked crust,
squeezed and broken up with a
fork). Season, add herbs.

Spread this mixture on to
the mushrooms, dot with butter
and set them on a baking sheet,
or in an ovenproof dish. Bake for
12–15 minutes in an oven at
400°F or Mark 7, and serve in
the ovenproof dish.

Buttered marrow

1 marrow
1–2 oz butter
salt and pepper
parsley (chopped)

Method

Peel the marrow, remove seeds
and cut into 2-inch squares.
Melt butter in a large shallow
pan and add marrow. Season
and cover with buttered paper
and a lid. Cook over gentle heat
until tender, shaking the pan
from time to time. Allow 15–20
minutes cooking time and
garnish with chopped parsley.

Fried onions

1 medium-size onion per person
2–3 tablespoons dripping, or oil
sugar (for dusting)

Method

Peel onion, slice a small piece
off the side so that the onion
remains firmly on the chopping
board while slicing fairly finely
across (not lengthways). Push
stalks of slices out into rings.

To make onions more digestible, blanch after slicing by
putting into cold water and
bringing to the boil. Refresh by
pouring cold water over and
draining well on absorbent
paper.

Put slices into the frying pan
with smoking hot fat or oil and
fry fairly quickly, turning occasionally with a fork. Dust with
sugar to help them brown.
When well browned take out
and drain on absorbent paper
before serving in heaps around,
or on top of, steaks.

To peel onions

First cut off top and root
with a sharp knife, then
peel off first and second
skins, or more (until onion
is all white). Do not break
the thin underskin—the
oil released from here will
make you cry.

To skin button onions
easily, first scald (plunge
into boiling water) for 1–2
minutes, then plunge into
cold water.

Buttered courgettes

7–8 courgettes (according to size)
1–1½ oz butter
1 tablespoon water
salt and pepper
½ tablespoon chopped parsley
½ tablespoon chopped fresh mixed
    herbs (optional)

Method

Wipe and trim stalks of courgettes; blanch them if large and
firm, otherwise put directly into
a pan or a flameproof casserole
with butter and 1 tablespoon of
water.

Add seasoning and press
buttered paper on top; cover
with a lid (to conserve all
juices). Cook slowly on top of
stove for 15-20 minutes, or
until tender. Garnish with
chopped herbs.

Sauté potatoes

1½ lb potatoes
2 tablespoons oil
1 oz butter
salt and pepper
1 dessertspoon chopped parsley

Method

Scrub potatoes and boil in their
skins until very tender. Then
drain, peel and slice. After heating a frying pan put in oil, and
when this is hot add the butter.
Slip in all the potatoes at once,
add seasoning and cook (sauté)
until golden-brown and crisp,
yet buttery, occasionally turning the contents of the pan.
Draw aside, check seasoning,
and add parsley. Serve in a very
hot dish.

Sauté cucumber

1 large cucumber
½–1 oz butter
1 bunch spring onions (trimmed),
    or 1 small onion (chopped)
salt and pepper
fresh mint (chopped) – to garnish

Method

Peel cucumber using a stainless
steel knife; split in four lengthways. Cut across into 1-inch
chunks, blanch in boiling, salted
water for 1 minute, then drain
well. Melt butter in a pan, add
spring onions (or chopped
onion). Cover and cook for 1
minute. Add cucumber, season.
Cover and cook for 5–6
minutes or until just tender,
occasionally shaking pan
gently. Garnish with fresh mint.
Watchpoint Do not overcook or cucumber will become
watery and tasteless.

Baked (roast) potatoes

Choose medium to large potatoes of even size. Peel and blanch by putting into cold salted water and bringing to the boil. Drain thoroughly and lightly scratch the surface with a fork (this will prevent a dry and leathery exterior after cooking). Now put the potatoes into smoking hot fat in the same tin as the meat which is roasting, 40–45 minutes before the meat is fully cooked, and baste well. Cook until soft (test by piercing with a cooking fork or fine skewer), basting them when you baste the meat and turning after 25 minutes. Drain well on kitchen paper, pile in a vegetable dish and sprinkle with a little salt. Do not cover before serving.

Glazed carrots

1–2 lb carrots
1 teaspoon sugar
1 oz butter
salt
mint (chopped)

Method

Peel carrots, leave whole, or quarter if small. If very large, cut in thin slices. Put in a pan with water to cover, sugar, butter and a pinch of salt. Cover and cook steadily until tender, then remove lid and cook until all the water has evaporated when the butter and sugar will form a glaze round the carrots.

Add a little chopped mint just before serving.

Cabbage

Cabbage is the most English — and most maligned — of all vegetables. To overcome this reputation every Cordon Bleu cook must remember the following golden rules:
1 Cabbage, like all vegetables that grow above the ground, when plain boiled must be put into plenty of boiling salted water and cooked uncovered.
2 Remove coarser outer leaves. Do not make a cut in stem base because this will spoil the shape and allow juices to escape. Wash well in several waters.
3 Avoid overcooking. For plain boiling, 10–12 minutes is enough. Although the cabbage must be tender, it should still have a certain bite and crispness. After draining, finish cooking in butter.
4 Avoid keeping cabbage hot for any length of time because this will give it an unpleasant smell and spoil the colour. Cook it early, by all means, but when tender tip into a colander, drain and rinse well with cold water. This will set the bright green colour. When the meal is nearly ready, turn the cabbage into a large shallow pan, heat quickly until steam stops rising, then add $\frac{1}{2}$–1 oz butter in small pieces and toss until melted. Season and serve.

Braised cabbage

1 firm white cabbage
1 large onion
1 oz butter
1 cooking apple (peeled and sliced)
salt and pepper
1–2 tablespoons stock

Method

Cut the cabbage in quarters and cut away the core. Shred finely. If you are using hard white Dutch cabbage, blanch by putting into boiling salted water for 1 minute, draining and refreshing with 1 cup of cold water. This is not necessary for green cabbage. Slice the onion and put in a flameproof casserole with the butter. Cook over gentle heat until soft but not coloured. Add the cabbage to the pan with the peeled and sliced apple. Season, stir well and pour in the stock. Cover with non-stick (silicone) cooking paper and lid, and cook for 45–50 minutes on the bottom shelf of the oven at 325°F or Mark 3.

Creamed swedes

These should not be dismissed as something nasty remembered from schooldays. Try swedes this way and give them a chance.

1 lb swedes
1 oz butter
black pepper
1 small carton double cream

Method

Peel swedes, cut into even-size wedges and cook in salted water until tender. Drain well and return to the heat to dry. Crush with a potato masher or fork, add the butter and continue cooking over gentle heat until all the water has gone. Season and pour in the cream just before serving the swedes.

Petits pois à la francaise

1 packet of A.F.D. peas
4 outside leaves of lettuce (finely shredded)
6 spring onions (cut in pieces)
1 oz butter
1 tablespoon flour

Method

Follow the cooking instructions on the packet of peas, adding the lettuce leaves and spring onions. When peas are tender, add just enough kneaded butter (made from butter and flour) in small pieces to bind peas, lettuce and liquid together.

Jardinière platter

1½ lb carrots
1½ lb small brussels sprouts
(trimmed)
1 lb small pickling onions
(skinned)
2 lb jerusalem artichokes (peeled),
or 1 lb courgettes
½ lb button mushrooms
2 cauliflowers

For serving
1 teaspoon sugar (for carrots)
1 teaspoon chopped mint (for
carrots)
4¼ oz butter
2 teaspoons sugar (for onions)
slice of lemon (for artichokes)
juice of ½ small lemon
salt and pepper
1 dessertspoon chopped parsley

The vegetables are all cooked separately and then arranged together on a large serving platter. Serve with roast meat.

Method
Carrots
Peel and quarter lengthways. Cover with cold water and add 1 teaspoon sugar, a pinch of salt, ½ oz butter, and cook until tender and all the water has evaporated (about 15 minutes). Add 1 teaspoon chopped mint before serving.

Brussels sprouts
Cook until just tender in boiling salted water for about 8 minutes, drain and toss in ¼ oz butter.

Pickling onions
Cover with cold water and bring to the boil – drain well. Return to the pan with 1 oz butter, 2 teaspoons sugar; cover and cook slowly until they are brown and sticky. Shake the pan from time to time and turn the onions. They should be tender after 8–10 minutes' cooking, but this does depend on the speed of cooking.

Jerusalem artichokes
Cut into even-size pieces after peeling and cook in boiling salted water with a slice of lemon to help keep their colour and to give flavour. When tender, drain artichokes well and add ½ oz butter to the pan with pepper ground from the mill and a little extra salt to season.

Courgettes
Thickly slice and blanch the courgettes in boiling water for 1 minute. Drain and return to the pan with ½ oz butter, cover pan tightly and cook until tender for about 8–10 minutes.

Mushrooms
Wash and trim the mushrooms and put them on a well-buttered ovenproof plate. Season with salt, pepper and a squeeze of lemon juice, cover with buttered paper and a pan lid or a second ovenproof plate and cook for about 10 minutes in an oven at 400°F or Mark 6.

Cauliflower
Divide the cauliflower into sprigs and, using a potato peeler, remove the outside skin on the stalk of the cauliflower sprigs. Cook in boiling salted water until just tender (about 5 minutes) and drain well.

To dish up, arrange the vegetables in rows in a large ▶

Jardinière platter continued

hot serving platter. Melt 1½ oz butter in a small pan and cook slowly until a nut-brown, add squeeze of lemon juice, salt and pepper and the chopped parsley. Pour this butter, while it is still foaming, over the vegetables, particularly the artichokes (or courgettes) and the cauliflower.

Eggs

How to cook eggs

Boiled eggs
(oeufs à la coque)

There is quite an art in boiling an egg – though many people still say that if they can't cook, they can at least boil an egg! However, many things can go wrong: the white may be runny, the yolk too set, or worst of all, the shell may crack in the water so that most of the white escapes.

Points given here should help you avoid these pitfalls. One answer is, of course, an egg-timer – but don't, like a young bride we knew, put the timer in the pan with the egg.

1 Make sure that the shells are perfectly clean. If not, wash or wipe with a damp cloth.
2 Choose an enamel pan for boiling eggs because they will blacken an aluminium one. If an aluminium pan has to be used, a little vinegar added to the water will prevent this. Vinegar will also prevent the white seeping away if the eggs crack, which is especially likely with preserved eggs.
3 Never take the eggs straight from a refrigerator or cold larder. Leave eggs at room temperature for a while, so that they are warm, before putting them into boiling salted water.
4 Boil eggs steadily but gently for $3\frac{1}{2}$-4 minutes according to taste. Allow $3\frac{1}{2}$ minutes for a lightly-boiled egg, and 4 minutes for one that is well set. Take the time from when the water reboils after adding them to pan.

It is generally reckoned that the slower the white cooks, the more digestible the egg. In this case, put the eggs into a pan of cold water and bring them slowly to the boil. Allow a further 30 seconds of gentle simmering, when the eggs will be lightly cooked.

Coddled eggs

Put into a pan of boiling water, cover, take off heat and leave for 5 minutes. Eggs cooked in this way will have a soft, creamy white and are ideal for children and invalids.

To make sure egg is cooked if you have no timer, an old-fashioned trick is to lift the egg from the water and count eight. If the shell becomes dry, the egg is coddled.

Soft-boiled eggs
(oeufs mollets)

Many dishes, both hot and cold, can be made from soft-boiled eggs. For these dishes the eggs are cooked a little differently.

1 Put them into a pan of boiling water and allow 5 minutes from time water comes back to the boil. Remember, though, that a small egg will take less time to cook through.
2 Take them out at once and put into cold water for 7–8 minutes. Then peel carefully.
3 The eggs may be used straight away. If you want them hot, they may be put (unpeeled) into hand-hot water for 5 minutes. If you want them cold, peel and leave in cold water for several hours until required.

As these eggs are delicate to peel, first crack the shells gently all over with the back of a spoon. This will soften the shell and make it easier to take off without breaking the egg. Once cracked all over, peel off a band across the middle of the egg. You will then find that the shell at each end of the egg can be pulled off.

Hard-boiled eggs
(oeufs durs)

Always put them in boiling water and allow 10–12 minutes steady boiling, but no longer, because over-boiling discolours the yolks and toughens the whites. Plunge them at once into cold water, which will make the eggs easier to peel, however fresh they are. Peel as for soft-boiled eggs.

To stuff hard-boiled eggs: cut them lengthways after peeling and scoop out the yolks with the handle of a teaspoon. Put the whites at once into a bowl of cold water to keep them tender and white.

When required, carefully lift out whites and lay them, cut side downwards, on a clean cloth to drain. If serving cold stuffed eggs, it is easier if the halved whites are arranged in place on the serving dish before filling with the prepared mixture. This will give a better and neater result. Stick them to the surface of the dish with a little of the filling.

Once the halved whites are filled, an alternative way of dishing them up is to put them together to reshape the egg. Dish up as for the halved whites. If serving boiled eggs under a sauce, especially if it has to be glazed or browned, the eggs should be slightly softer. Before coating them with a sauce, dry eggs well on

absorbent paper or a cloth, otherwise the sauce will slide off. Be sure, too, that the sauce, particularly mayonnaise, is of a good coating consistency.

Buttered or scrambled eggs
(oeufs brouillés)

These should be soft, creamy and melting and this depends largely on the amount of butter added. Don't add too much milk as this is inclined to give a curdled, watery effect.

To 4 eggs allow 1 good oz of butter and 3 tablespoons of single cream or creamy milk. Beat eggs well with a fork, adding milk, salt and pepper and half butter in small pieces.

Melt remaining butter in a pan, pour in the egg mixture and cook over moderate heat, stirring and scraping the mixture from the bottom of the pan with a spoon, preferably metal, to get thick, creamy flakes. Take care not to overcook eggs. Turn them on to buttered toast while they are still creamy.

Here's an alternative way for those who do not like too rich a mixture. Put the butter and milk into the pan first (here a little more milk may be used) and, when hot, break in the eggs and allow the white to set lightly before stirring. Then season and stir mixture to break up eggs and continue cooking until the scrambled eggs are thick.

Fried eggs
(oeufs frits)

You can fry these eggs in ▶ 51

either shallow or deep fat.

Shallow frying: make sure that the fat (not less than $\frac{1}{4}$ inch in the pan) is not too hot. If it is, it will toughen the whites. Break the eggs, one at a time, into a cup and gently slide them into the pan. Cook on moderate heat, basting with the fat, until both white and yolk are set. To speed the process, the pan may be put under a hot grill for a few seconds.

Deep fat frying: half fill a small deep pan with fat; heat until 400°F (oil to 360°–375°F–see page 143). Gently tip in the eggs and cook for 2–3 minutes until golden-brown. Drain the eggs very carefully. For the best results, do not fry more than two at a time.

Poached eggs
(oeufs pochés)

New-laid eggs are best for poaching, otherwise the white will detach itself from the yolk. Poach eggs in a saucepan or deep frying pan filled with boiling water – add about 1 tablespoon vinegar to 1 quart of water. Do not add salt as this tends to toughen the white.

Keep heat low and water gently simmering, then break eggs into pan and poach for about $3\frac{1}{2}$–$4\frac{1}{2}$ minutes until firm. Lift out with a draining spoon or fish slice and drain thoroughly before dishing up.

Egg poachers are available but the above method is satisfactory as the eggs do not stick (which sometimes happens in a poacher) and are less obviously 'moulded' in shape.

Poached eggs, like soft-boiled eggs, can be kept several hours in water before use. To reheat the eggs, lift into a bowl of hand-hot water and leave 4–5 minutes before taking them out and draining.

For cold poached eggs the whites must be really firm; the yolks should just give under gentle pressure.

For hot poached eggs to be served under a sauce, especially if it has to be glazed or browned, the eggs should be slightly softer. Dry eggs well on absorbent paper or cloth before dishing and coating with a sauce, otherwise the sauce will slide off.

Baked eggs
(shirred eggs – oeufs en cocotte or sur-le-plat)

These are delicious and may be cooked and served in individual buttered cocottes, ramekins or soufflé dishes or in a shallow ovenproof dish.

In their simplest form they have a little melted butter and cream, or creamy milk, poured over the yolks after the eggs have been broken into a buttered and seasoned dish. They are then baked in the oven at 350°–375°F or Mark 4–5 for 6–8 minutes.

For a more substantial dish and an excellent way of using up leftovers, just break eggs on to a savoury mixture.

Watchpoint Do not overcook as eggs will continue cooking after the dish has been removed from the oven.

How to make omelets

An omelet, one of the most useful egg dishes, is quick, quite easy to make and delicious whether plain or stuffed. The secret lies in using really fresh eggs and a good omelet pan, which should be kept for omelets only. If the pan is used for frying other foods, it has to be washed, which can cause food to stick.

A true omelet pan is made either of thick aluminium or cast iron, with or without a non-stick finish. The characteristic of the pan is its curved edge, which makes the omelet easier to turn out and gives it a better shape.

Pans come in different sizes, but a 7–8 inch diameter one is a good size and will take 3–4 eggs, which are usually enough for two people. A large, heavy pan is more awkward to handle and the omelet itself is not easy to manipulate.

When buying an omelet pan, treat it before use as follows: wash it well, dry and cover the bottom with salad oil. Leave for at least 12 hours, then heat oil to frying point; remove from heat, pour off oil and wipe pan thoroughly with absorbent paper. The inside of the pan should not be washed after each use, but wiped with a damp cloth dipped in salt. This will season the pan and prevent an omelet from sticking.

Plain omelet

4 eggs
1½ tablespoons cold water
salt
black pepper (ground from mill)
1 oz butter

7-8 inch diameter omelet pan

Method

Break eggs into a basin and beat well with a fork. When well mixed, add water and seasoning (this should be done just before making it). Heat pan on medium heat. Put in butter in two pieces and, when frothing, pour in egg mixture at once. Leave 10–15 seconds before stirring round slowly with the flat of a fork. Do this once or twice, stop and leave for another 5–6 seconds.

Lift up edge of omelet to let any remaining raw egg run on to hot pan. Now tilt pan away from you and fold over omelet to far side. Change your grip on pan so that the handle runs up the palm of your hand. Take the hot dish or plate, in your other hand, tilt it slightly and tip omelet on to it. Serve at once.

Herb omelet
(Fines herbes omelet)

This is especially delicious in summer when herbs are fresh.

Method

Make as for a plain 4-egg omelet and add 1 rounded tablespoon of mixed chopped herbs (parsley, thyme, marjoram or tarragon, and chives) before pouring mixture into pan.

Snip chives finely with scissors rather than chopping them. The mixture should be quite green with the herbs.

Chicken liver omelet

2–3 chicken livers
¼ oz butter
flour (for dusting)
dash of sherry
stock (to moisten)
½ teaspoon tomato purée (optional)

Method

Sauté chicken livers in butter in a pan; then slice and dust with flour. Add a dash of sherry and moisten with a little stock. Bring to boil and simmer for 2–3 minutes. Add tomato purée. Make a plain omelet, spoon in mixture before folding over.

Bacon and potato omelet

2–3 rashers of bacon
2 medium-size potatoes (diced)
1 small onion (finely sliced)
¼ oz butter
salt and pepper

Method

Cut bacon across into strips. Melt butter in pan, add potatoes, onion and bacon. Season, cover pan and cook slowly for 7–8 minutes, or until potatoes and onion are tender and slightly brown. Stir occasionally.

Make plain omelet, spoon in mixture before folding over.

Cheese omelet

Make as for a plain 4-egg omelet and scatter 2–3 tablespoons grated cheese thickly over omelet whilst in pan, just before folding it over. A mature cheddar or Gruyère is best.

Spanish omelet

5 eggs (well beaten)
5 tablespoons olive oil
3 oz raw lean ham, or gammon
  rasher (chopped)
1 Spanish onion (thinly sliced)
1 clove of garlic (crushed with
  ½ teaspoon salt) – optional
6 oz (about 2–3) potatoes (sliced,
  or coarsely grated)
salt and pepper

A true Spanish omelet is made on a base of potatoes and onion, then cooked in olive oil and well flavoured with garlic. Another version includes cooked mixed vegetables and is good for making use of leftovers. The consistency of both these omelets is firm, but not too solid. It is cut into wedges, like a cake, for serving.

Method

Heat the oil in a frying pan, add the ham, or gammon, cook for a few minutes, then add the onion and a little of the crushed garlic to taste, if wished. Fry gently until the onion is half cooked, then add the potato. Season well; cook until soft.

Drain off any superfluous oil and add beaten eggs to pan. Stir to mix, then cook until the underneath of omelet is brown. When the mixture is barely set, slide the pan under the grill to brown the top surface. When well browned, turn out omelet on to a flat dish.

Cut into wedges to serve.

How to make hot soufflés

Hot soufflés are often consider-
ed to be the test of a good cook.
They are not difficult to make if
you follow the basic rules but, as
with all tests of skill, circum-
stances must be right. Don't
serve a savoury soufflé as a first
course for a luncheon or dinner
party unless you know your
guests are going to be punctual.
However, for everyday family
meals, you can experiment with
a variety of soufflés.

Rules for making sweet or savoury soufflés

1 Choose the right size soufflé
dish or case for the quantity of
mixture being made. Dishes are
generally numbered 1–3, and
the equivalent diameters are
given in recipes overleaf (except
for No. 3 which has a 5$\frac{1}{2}$-inch
diameter top). Before baking,
dish should be two-thirds to
three-quarters full of mixture.

2 Prepare the dish by rubbing
the inside lightly with butter, and
in the case of savoury soufflés
dust with browned crumbs as
it will then be easier to clean.

3 To allow the soufflé to rise
2–3 inches above the dish when
baked, cut a band or strip of
doubled greaseproof paper,
about 6–7 inches wide, and
long enough to overlap some
3 inches round the side of dish.
Make a 2-inch fold along one
long side. Butter the strip above
this fold, and wrap the band
round the outside of the dish,
the folded piece at the base and
turned inwards. This will keep
the paper upright and firm.
The greased section of the paper

*Having rubbed inside of dish with
butter, for savoury soufflé dust
with browned crumbs; wrap greaseproof paper band round with a 2-inch
fold at base and a 3-inch overlap*

*Tying paper band round to stand 2–3
inches above the rim of the dish*

should stand above dish by some 3 inches.

Tie paper securely with string and set the dish on a baking sheet before filling. The string should be untied and the paper peeled off just before serving.

4 It is the whipped egg whites that make a soufflé rise, so it is important to whip them well. Ideally you should use a copper bowl and a light wire whisk. Whisking by hand in a bowl of this shape (see photograph below) gives more bulk to whites. If you do not have a copper bowl, use a wire whisk with a china or earthenware bowl. Don't use a rotary whisk or mixer.

5 When adding egg whites to the mixture, stir in a small quantity with a metal spoon before the main bulk is added. This first addition softens the mixture so that once the remaining whites are added the whole remains light and fluffy.

6 Pre-heat the oven to 375°F or Mark 5. Arrange the shelves so that the soufflé can be placed in the centre of the oven, with no shelf above it. This will give it plenty of room to rise. To avoid any unnecessary opening of oven door, try not to cook anything else when a soufflé is in the oven.

7 A soufflé should be served immediately from the oven. Better to keep the family waiting than the soufflé. When cooked the top should be evenly brown and firm to the touch (approximate cooking times are given in individual recipes), and the consistency lightly firm, with the centre soft and creamy.

8 Hot soufflés benefit by the addition of 1 extra white to yolks. Though this is not essential it makes for a lighter and fluffier mixture.

A little of the egg white is first folded in to soften the mixture

Cheese soufflé

4 rounded tablespoons grated cheese
1½ oz butter
1 rounded tablespoon flour
salt
cayenne pepper
¾ cup of milk
1 teaspoon ready-made mustard
4 egg yolks
5 egg whites
1 tablespoon browned crumbs

7-inch diameter top (size No. 1) soufflé dish

Ideally the cheese used should be a mixture of grated Parmesan and Gruyère. Otherwise use a dry Cheddar.

Method

First prepare soufflé dish. Set oven at 375°F or Mark 5.

Choose a medium to large saucepan. Make a roux by melting the butter, removing pan from heat and stirring in the flour. Season well, blend in milk. Put pan back on heat, stir until boiling then draw aside. Add mustard and beat in 3 rounded tablespoons cheese and egg yolks one at a time.

When well mixed whip egg whites to a firm snow, stir 2 tablespoons of the whites into the sauce, using a metal spoon. Then stir in the remainder in two parts, lifting the sauce well over the whites from the bottom of the pan. Turn the bowl round while mixing; do not overmix.

Turn lightly into prepared soufflé dish. Quickly dust top with crumbs and rest of cheese mixed together. Bake for 25–30 minutes in pre-set oven, until evenly brown and firm to the touch. Serve immediately.

Orange soufflé

3 oz lump sugar (about 18 lumps)
2 oranges
½ pint milk
1 rounded tablespoon flour
1 oz butter
3 egg yolks
4 egg whites
little sifted icing sugar

7-inch diameter top (size No. 1) soufflé dish

Method

Prepare soufflé dish. Set oven at 375°F or Mark 5.

Rub some of the lumps of sugar over the outside rind of the oranges until they are soaked with the oil (zest). Then set aside.

Mix 3 tablespoons of the milk with the flour until smooth. Scald remaining milk, add all the sugar lumps and cover. Leave to infuse for 5–7 minutes off the heat. Then return pan to heat. Add the flour mixture gradually and stir until boiling. Boil 2–3 seconds, then draw aside and dot the surface with the butter. Cover and leave for 5 minutes.

Beat in egg yolks, one at a time. Whip whites to a firm snow, stir in 1 tablespoon, then cut and stir in remainder, using a metal spoon. Turn at once into prepared dish and bake in pre-set oven for about 18–20 minutes or until well risen.

Then draw out oven shelf with soufflé on it, dust top quickly with icing sugar and return shelf. Cook for a further 4–5 minutes to caramelise the top. Serve at once.

Soufflé omelets

These are usually served as a sweet and can have various fillings. The mixture may be cooked in an omelet pan on top of the stove, or in a soufflé or ovenproof dish in the oven.

Jam omelet

4 large eggs (separated)
1 tablespoon caster sugar
2 tablespoons single cream, or creamy milk
apricot, or strawberry, or gooseberry jam (preferably home-made)
½ oz butter
little sifted icing sugar

2–3 metal skewers; 8-inch diameter omelet pan

Other fillings which may be used are fresh sliced strawberries mixed with 1 tablespoon of warm redcurrant jelly, or 2–3 bananas sliced and sautéed in a little butter, and then well dusted with caster sugar and sprinkled with lemon juice.

Method

Mix egg yolks with the sugar and cream. Warm 2–3 tablespoons of the jam in a small saucepan. Whip whites to a firm snow and cut and fold into the yolk mixture, using a metal spoon. Set oven at 400°F or Mark 6 or turn on grill. Heat omelet pan until moderately hot, and put skewers in flame or under grill until red hot.

Drop butter into the pan and, while still foaming, put in the egg mixture. Spread out in the pan and cook on moderate heat for less than 1 minute to allow the bottom to brown. Do not stir during this time.

Then slide pan into pre-set oven or under the grill to set the top. Spread omelet quickly with jam or other filling, fold over with a palette knife; turn or slide on to a hot dish, dredge with icing sugar and mark a lattice across the top with red-hot skewers. (Heat several skewers at a time rather than heating them one by one.)

Note: marking soufflé omelets with red-hot skewers gives a traditional finish and a pleasant taste of caramel; otherwise just dust the omelet with caster, instead of icing, sugar.

Slide omelet on to a warm dish or plate and flip over with knife

Cold sweet mousses and soufflés

A cold sweet mousse is made with whole eggs plus extra egg yolks beaten together with sugar until thick, flavouring in the form of purée added, and the whole enriched with cream and lightly set with gelatine.

For a cold sweet soufflé, the eggs are always separated, the yolks are beaten with the sugar and flavouring (in the form of juice or purée) until thick, or made into a custard with milk when cream is added. Stiffly whisked egg whites are folded in to give it the characteristic soufflé texture and the whole is lightly set with melted gelatine. The soufflé dish should be prepared as on page 56.

Caramel mousse

6 oz lump, or granulated, sugar
$\frac{1}{4}$ pint water
2 egg yolks
3 eggs
2 oz caster sugar
$\frac{1}{4}$ pint double cream
juice of 1 lemon
scant $\frac{1}{2}$ oz gelatine

Ring mould (1 $\frac{1}{2}$ pints capacity)

Method

Lightly oil the mould. Put the lump sugar and half the water into a heavy pan and, when dissolved, cook steadily to a rich brown caramel. Use a cloth to cover the hand holding the saucepan (to avoid splashes) and add the rest of the cold water. Stir until caramel is melted, pour into a bowl and leave it to cool. Whisk the egg yolks and whole eggs with caster sugar over gentle heat until very thick and mousse-like (or use an electric mixer without heat). Remove from heat and whisk until quite cold.

Lightly whip half the cream, add to the mousse with the caramel and set the bowl in a second one containing water and ice cubes.

Make the lemon juice up to $2\frac{1}{2}$ fl oz with water, if necessary. Dissolve the gelatine in this over heat. Stir gelatine liquid into the mousse until the mixture begins to thicken, then pour into the mould and leave mousse in a cool place to set.

Turn out the mousse and decorate with the remaining cream. The centre may be filled with fresh raspberries or strawberries when in season.

Gooseberry soufflé

$\frac{1}{2}$ pint gooseberry purée (made with 1 lb green gooseberries, $\frac{1}{4}$ pint water, 4 rounded table-spoons granulated sugar)
4 eggs (separated)
2 oz caster sugar
$\frac{1}{4}$ pint double cream
$\frac{1}{2}$ oz gelatine
5 tablespoons water
2–3 drops of green colouring (optional)

For decoration
7 fl oz double cream (whipped)
browned almonds (finely chopped), or crushed ratafia crumbs

6-inch diameter top (size No. 2) soufflé dish

Method

Prepare soufflé dish.

Beat egg yolks, sugar and purée in a bowl. Whisk mixture over heat until it is thick, then remove from heat and continue whisking until bowl is cool (heat is not necessary if using an electric mixer).

Half whip the $\frac{1}{4}$ pint cream, stir into gooseberry mixture. Soak gelatine in water, then dissolve over gentle heat; add to soufflé with colouring. When mixture begins to thicken, whisk egg whites to a firm snow, fold in carefully and turn soufflé into dish; leave it to set.

Decorate with whipped cream and the nuts or ratafia crumbs.

How to make custards

There are two types of custard. The first is when eggs and milk are mixed together and baked, or steamed, to set to a firm consistency, eg. as for caramel custard. The second type of custard is when egg yolks and milk are cooked over a gentle heat to a creamy consistency. This is a soft custard and often forms the basis of cold creams and soufflés set with gelatine.

Important points to note: Egg whites will set a custard and egg yolks will give it a creamy consistency. For a cooked custard, eg. baked or steamed, the proportion of eggs to milk should be 2 whole eggs and 2 egg yolks to 1 pint of milk. For a soft custard take 4 egg yolks to 1 pint of milk. More yolks can be added if a very rich custard is called for. Whites tend to curdle the mixture. Eggs and milk will curdle if allowed to get too hot. For baking a custard in the oven, it is wise to use a bain marie. For a soft custard scald milk by bringing up to boiling point. You can use a double saucepan, the lower pan containing hot water, but if care is taken, the custard can be thickened on direct, but gentle heat. When eggs are scarce, 1 teaspoon of cornflour can replace 1 egg yolk in a custard sauce.

Cooking 'au bain marie'

This term is used to describe a method of cooking in the oven (custards, creams, etc.), as opposed to keeping sauces, etc. hot in a bain marie or double boiler on top of the stove.

A large tin, such as a roasting tin, is half filled with hot water and the dish or mould placed in the centre. The tin with its contents is then lifted into the oven and left to cook for the appropriate time. This protects the mixture from the direct oven heat which might cause curdling. Unless you want to brown the top, eg. a custard pudding, cover the top of dish in the bain marie with a piece of foil or buttered greaseproof paper while cooking.

Vanilla pods give a particularly delicate flavour to custard or cream. These pods can be bought separately and used several times over. Little white crystals on the pod indicate its freshness.

The seeds hold most of the flavour, so it is best to split pod and scrape out some of the tiny black seeds to use with it. Once used rinse pod in warm water, allow to dry before putting away in a small jar of caster sugar. Keep well stoppered; this vanilla sugar may be used for flavouring cakes and custards.

Custard sauce
(Crème à la vanille)

$\frac{1}{2}$ pint creamy milk
2 tablespoons caster sugar
2–3 drops of vanilla essence, or
  $\frac{1}{2}$ vanilla pod (split)
2 egg yolks

Method

Put the milk in a pan, add the sugar with vanilla essence or, if using a vanilla pod, infuse it in milk for 10 minutes, keeping pan covered. Take out pod, then add sugar.

Cream the yolks in a bowl, bring the milk to scalding point and pour on gradually. Blend mixture together and return to the pan; stir continually over a gentle heat with a wooden spatula or spoon. Stir gently to avoid splashing. When the custard coats the spoon and looks creamy, strain back into the bowl.

Dredge a little caster sugar over the top and leave to cool. This coating of sugar melts and helps prevent a skin forming.
Watchpoint Should the custard get too hot and begin to curdle, turn at once into the basin without straining and whisk briskly for 2–3 seconds. Remember that gentle heat helps to prevent a custard from curdling and makes it creamier.

Petits pots de crème (Small pots of cream)

1½ pints milk
vanilla pod
3 eggs
3 egg yolks
1 tablespoon vanilla sugar (see
  page 62)
2 tablespoons caster sugar
2 teaspoons instant coffee
2 oz plain chocolate

deep mousse pots, or ramekin pots

Method

Warm all the milk with the vanilla pod, remove from heat and leave to infuse 5–10 minutes until well flavoured. Meanwhile, break 1 of the eggs into a bowl, add 1 yolk and 1 tablespoon vanilla sugar, and beat well with a fork, but do not allow to get frothy. Remove the vanilla pod from milk, and pour ½ pint on to eggs and sugar. Blend well, strain and pour into pots.

Using the same bowl, beat 1 egg, 1 egg yolk and 1 tablespoon caster sugar. Warm the remaining milk slightly, and pour ½ pint of it on to eggs and sugar. Blend in the coffee, making sure it has thoroughly dissolved, strain and pour into pots.

Again using the same bowl (any leftover coffee will improve the flavour of the chocolate), beat the remaining egg, egg yolk and sugar. Simmer the chocolate in remaining ½ pint milk for 2–3 minutes. Pour on to the eggs and sugar, blend, strain and pour into pots.

Place the filled pots in water in a bain marie, or in a deep ovenproof dish on a baking sheet, covered with buttered paper. Cook in oven at 350°F–375°F or Mark 4–5 for 12–15 minutes until just set. Take out and chill. Serve plain or with cream.

Caramel cream (Crème caramel)

1 pint milk
2 eggs
2 egg yolks
1½ tablespoons caster sugar

For caramel
4 oz lump, or granulated, sugar
½ cup water

6-inch diameter soufflé dish, or cake tin

Method

Scald milk. Break eggs into a bowl, then add the extra yolks. Beat well with a fork but do not allow to get frothy. Add sugar and milk, mix, set aside.

Put sugar and water for caramel into a small pan, dissolve sugar over a gentle heat, then boil rapidly without stirring until a rich brown in colour. Stop boiling by dipping bottom of pan into a basin of cold water and, when still, pour three-quarters of caramel into a dry and warm soufflé dish or cake tin; pour rest on to an oiled plate or tin. Turn soufflé dish or cake tin carefully round to coat the caramel evenly over the bottom and sides.

Strain in the custard mixture, cover with foil or a piece of buttered paper. Cook in a bain marie in the oven at 375°F or Mark 5 for 40–50 minutes until just set; take out and leave until cool before turning out. Crush the rest of the caramel and put round the dish.

Watchpoint A certain amount of caramel will always be left in the mould after turning out; this can be lessened by adding 1 teaspoon boiling water to caramel before pouring it into soufflé dish or cake tin. For a more creamy-textured result, use an extra egg yolk.

Coat caramel round sides of the dish, then strain in the custard

Stocks

As every good cook knows, the best casseroles, stews, braises and
sauces owe their fine flavour to the original stock. Poor stock can
turn a promising dish into a dull and tasteless mixture. If a recipe
calls for good stock and you don't have any to hand (nor feel like
making some), then *change your choice of dish*. Trying to
compromise can lead to failure in making a special dish.
Most larders have something – vegetables, carcass bones and so
on – which can be turned into a small quantity of stock for a
gravy or a simple sauce. If you want more, a few beef bones from
the butcher will make enough stock for a week for the average
family needs. Bones, on their own, will make a stronger stock
than if you use mixed vegetables and bits of meat (mixed stock).

Raw mutton bones and turnips are best left out of stocks unless
you are making a Scotch broth; both have a strong flavour and
could well spoil the dish for which the stock is intended.

The liquid in a stockpot should be reduced in quantity (by
simmering) by about a quarter, or even more, before the stock is
ready for straining.

In an emergency a bouillon cube can be used for certain things,
but it can never replace properly made stock because it will lack
the characteristic jellied quality. Bouillon cubes are salty and there
is always the danger of overdoing the seasoning.

Mixed stock

If you want a really clear stock, the only way to make it is to use raw bones. If you are using cooked ones as well, it helps to add these after the stock has come to the boil, although it is better not to mix raw with cooked bones if the stock is to be kept for any length of time.

Any trimmings or leftovers in the way of meat can go into your regular stockpot: chicken carcasses and giblets (but not the liver); bacon rinds; or a ham or bacon bone. This last is often given away and it makes excellent stock for a pea soup.

Add a plateful of cut-up root vegetables, a bouquet garni, 5–6 peppercorns, and pour in enough cold water to cover the ingredients by two-thirds. Salt very lightly, or not at all if there is a bacon bone in the pot. Bring slowly to the boil, skim, half-cover the pan and simmer 1½–2 hours or longer, depending on the quantity of stock being made. The liquid should reduce by about a third. Strain off and, when the stock is cold, skim well to remove any fat. Throw away the ingredients unless a fair amount of raw bones have been used, in which case more water can be added and a second boiling made.

If the stock is to be kept several days, or if there is a fair proportion of chicken in it, bring to the boil every day. If you are keeping it in the refrigerator, save room by storing, covered, in a jug instead of a bowl. Remember that the stronger the stock, the better it will keep.

Watchpoint Long slow simmering is essential for any meat stock. It should never be allowed to boil hard as this will result in a thick muddy-looking jelly instead of a semi-clear one.

'**Bouquet garni**' or bunch of herbs is traditionally made up of 2–3 parsley stalks, a sprig of thyme and bayleaf, tied with string if used in liquids which are later strained. Otherwise herbs are tied in a piece of muslin for easy removal before serving the dish.

Brown bone stock

3 lb beef bones (or mixed beef/veal)
2 onions (quartered)
2 carrots (quartered)
1 stick of celery
large bouquet garni
6 peppercorns
3–4 quarts water
salt

6-quart capacity saucepan, or small fish kettle

Method

Wipe bones but do not wash unless unavoidable. Put into a very large pan. Set on gentle heat and leave bones to fry gently for 15–20 minutes. Enough fat will come out from the marrow so do not add any to pan unless bones are very dry.

After 10 minutes add the vegetables, having sliced the celery into 3–4 pieces.

When bones and vegetables are just coloured, add herbs, peppercorns and the water, which should come up two-thirds above level of ingredients. Bring slowly to the boil, skimming occasionally, then half cover pan to allow reduction to take place and simmer 4–5 hours, or until stock tastes strong and good.

Strain off and use bones again for a second boiling. Although this second stock will not be so strong as the first, it is good for soups and gravies. Use the first stock for brown sauces, sautés, casseroles, or where a jellied stock is required. For a strong beef broth, add 1 lb shin of beef to the pot halfway through the cooking.

White bone stock

This stock forms a basis for cream sauces, white stews, etc. It is made in the same way as brown bone stock, except that bones and vegetables are not browned before the water is added, and veal bones are used. Do not add the vegetables until the bones have come to the boil and the fat has been skimmed off the liquid.

White bone stock (made only with veal bones) is a basis for cream sauces and white stews; don't brown the bones and vegetables

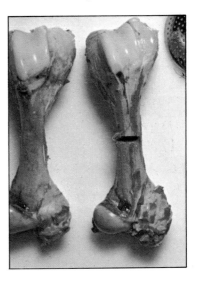

Vegetable stock

1 lb carrots
1 lb onions
½ head of celery
½ oz butter
3–4 peppercorns
1 teaspoon tomato purée
2 quarts water
salt

Method

Quarter vegetables, brown lightly in the butter in a large pan. Add peppercorns, tomato purée, water and salt. Bring to boil, cover pan and simmer 2 hours or until the stock has a good flavour.

To make bone stock in a pressure cooker, use either raw or cooked bones and root vegetables to flavour and put into the pan with enough water to cover. Salt lightly and add a few peppercorns. Bring to the boil, then cover and bring slowly to 15 lb pressure. Allow 40 minutes cooking time and cool at room temperature. Take off the cover and strain the stock, leave until cold, then re-move the fat. If using marrow bones (these make a particularly stiff jelly), ask your butcher to cut the bones reasonably small, add water to cover (but do not use vegetables) and a little salt and bring slowly to 15 lb pressure after allowing the liquid to boil first. Allow 2 hours of pressure cooking and then cool at room temperature. Strain and skim as before.

Chicken stock

This should ideally be made from the giblets (neck, gizzard, heart and feet, if available), but never the liver which imparts a bitter flavour. This is better kept for making paté, or sautéd and used as a savoury. Dry fry the giblets with an onion, washed but not peeled, and cut in half. To dry fry, use a thick pan with a lid, with barely enough fat to cover the bottom. Allow the pan to get very hot before putting in the giblets and onion, cook on full heat until lightly coloured. Remove pan from heat before covering with 2 pints of cold water. Add a large pinch of salt, a few peppercorns and a bouquet garni and simmer gently for 1–2 hours. Alternatively, make the stock when you roast a chicken by putting the giblets in the roasting tin around the chicken with the onion, herbs and 2 pints of water. This is preferable to bouillon cube stock for, in reducing the liquid with bouillon, there is the danger of the finished sauce being too salty.

Sauces

How to make white sauces

Points to remember

1 Weight of fat should be slightly more than that of flour to give a soft, semi-liquid roux, which is the foundation of a flour sauce.

2 If roux is hot, liquid should be warm or cold; if roux is cold, liquid must be warm. This makes blending easier and avoids a granular texture.

3 For a béchamel (or white) sauce, melt fat gently (do not let it sizzle), remove from heat and stir in flour (white roux). For a velouté sauce, cook flour in fat over a low heat for a few seconds until it is a pale straw colour (blond roux) before adding liquid.

4 Fats used may be butter, margarine, dripping or oil, according to the type of sauce being made.

Consistencies

The amount of flour to liquid in sauces can vary their consistencies for different uses:

Flowing. For serving as an accompanying sauce. Proportions: $\frac{1}{2}$ oz butter and just under $\frac{1}{2}$ oz flour to $\frac{1}{2}$ pint liquid.

Coating. Slightly thicker consistency for coating fillets of fish, eggs and vegetables. Proportions: $\frac{3}{4}$ oz butter and just under $\frac{3}{4}$ oz flour to $\frac{1}{2}$ pint liquid.

Panada. Thick sauce for binding, used as a base for croquettes, fish or meat creams. Proportions: $1\frac{1}{2}$–2 oz butter and just under $1\frac{1}{2}$–2 oz flour to $\frac{1}{2}$ pint liquid.

Liaisons

Liaisons play an important part in the making of sauces. The word means a binding together and is a term given to certain ingredients which are used to thicken sauces and soups.

There are various ways in which to bind sauces:

1 Kneaded butter (beurre manié) is a liaison mixture of butter and flour in the proportions of almost twice as much butter to flour, worked together on a plate with a fork to make a paste. It is added in small pieces to thicken liquid in which food has been cooked,eg. fish stews and casserole dishes. This is useful when the quantity of liquid remaining in a dish is unknown, making it difficult to know how much flour alone to use for thickening.

Kneaded butter should be added to hot (but not boiling) liquids. Shake pan gently and when the butter has dissolved (indicating flour has been absorbed in liquid), reboil. If the liquid is still not thick enough, the process can be repeated.

2 Fécule, ie. arrowroot or potato flour, should be slaked (mixed) with water or milk and stirred into the nearly boiling liquid off the heat. Once added, reboil and draw aside. Used for ragoûts and casseroles as well as brown sauces.

3 Egg yolks and cream. This mixture may be used to thicken and enrich velouté sauces and some cream soups. The yolk or yolks are worked well together with the cream. 2–3 tablespoons of sauce are blended into the mixture, a little at a time, and when well blended, the whole is returned to the main bulk of the sauce and stirred in gradually. Reheat, stirring continually, but do not boil. This will cook the egg yolks slowly and so give a particularly creamy consistency to the sauce.

Note: 1 rounded tablespoon, ie. as much above as below the rim, is equivalent to $\frac{1}{2}$ oz sifted flour. 1 level tablespoon equals $\frac{1}{4}$ oz sifted flour.

White sauce

$\frac{3}{4}$ oz butter
1 rounded tablespoon flour
$\frac{1}{2}$ pint milk
salt and pepper

A white sauce is quick and easy, made in exactly the same way and with same proportions as béchamel, but the milk is not flavoured. It can be used as the base for cheese, onion or other sauces with pronounced flavour, but béchamel is better for mushroom and egg sauces.

Method

Melt the butter in a small pan, remove from heat and stir in the flour. Blend in half the milk, then stir in the rest. Stir this over moderate heat until boiling, then boil gently for 1–2 minutes. Season to taste.

Béchamel sauce 1

½ pint milk
1 slice of onion
1 small bayleaf
6 peppercorns
1 blade of mace

For roux
¾ oz butter
1 rounded tablespoon flour
salt and pepper

Made on a white roux with flavoured milk added, béchamel can be used as a base for mornay (cheese), soubise (onion), mushroom or egg sauces. Proportions of ingredients may vary in these derivative sauces according to consistency required.

Method

Pour milk into a saucepan, add the flavourings, cover pan and infuse on gentle heat for 5–7 minutes. Strain milk and set it aside. Rinse and wipe out the pan and melt the butter in it. To give a white roux remove from heat before stirring in the flour. The roux must be soft.

Pour on half of milk through a strainer and blend until smooth using a wooden spoon, then add rest of milk. Season lightly, return to a slow to moderate heat and stir until boiling. Boil for no longer than 2 minutes.

Watchpoint If a flour sauce shows signs of lumps, these can be smoothed out by vigorous stirring or beating with a sauce whisk, provided sauce has not boiled; draw pan aside and stir vigorously. It can then be put back to boil gently for 1–2 minutes before using. If it has boiled and is still lumpy, the only remedy is to strain it.

Béchamel sauce

Louis de Béchamel, Marquis de Nointel, was Lord Steward of the Royal household to Louis XIV in the 17th century, and béchamel sauce is said to have been named after him rather than created by him. It is a major sauce and it forms the base for many others. In a béchamel, the milk is infused with spices to give a delicate and subtle flavour, unlike an ordinary white sauce. You may come across slight variations in the instructions for making béchamel sauces in different recipes, but we give the two basic methods, a short one and a longer one for a more subtle flavour.

Béchamel sauce 2

For mirepoix

1 small onion
1 small carrot
½ stick of celery
1 oz butter

For roux

1 oz butter
2 tablespoons flour
1 pint milk
bouquet garni
salt and pepper
pinch of grated nutmeg
1 tablespoon cream (optional)

Method

Dice the vegetables finely, and melt the butter in a large thick pan. Add this mirepoix of vegetables to the pan and press a piece of buttered paper down on top. Cover and cook gently for 8–10 minutes, but do not allow to colour. Now turn the mirepoix on to a plate.

Make the roux in the same pan, with one third of milk, and set aside. Scald remaining milk (by bringing quickly to the boil and removing from heat immediately) and pour on to the roux, whisking well at the same time. Add bouquet garni, seasoning and a little nutmeg.

Stir sauce over heat until it boils, then add mirepoix. Simmer in half-covered pan on low heat for 40 minutes, stirring from time to time. Then run the resulting sauce through a conical strainer, pressing lightly to remove juice from the mirepoix. Return to a clean pan for reheating. Add the cream (if used).

Mushroom sauce

2 oz mushrooms

For béchamel sauce

1 oz butter
1 rounded tablespoon flour
salt and pepper
½ pint flavoured milk (see basic recipe)

Serve with eggs, fish, chicken.

Method

Wash mushrooms, without peeling, and chop them. Cook mushrooms in half the butter for 2–3 minutes until fairly dry. Draw aside, add rest of butter and when melted stir in flour.

Season and blend in the milk. Stir until boiling and cook for 2 minutes.

Mornay (cheese) sauce

1–1½ oz (2–3 rounded tablespoons)
  grated cheese
½ teaspoon made mustard
  (French, or English)
½ pint well-seasoned white, or
  béchamel, sauce

Serve with eggs, fish, chicken and vegetables.

The cheese can be a mixture of Gruyère and Parmesan or a dry Cheddar. If using Gruyère, which thickens sauce, reduce basic roux to ½ oz each butter and flour (1 tablespoon). If too thick, add a little milk.

Method

Make white or béchamel sauce, remove from heat and gradually stir in grated cheese. When well mixed, add mustard. Reheat but do not boil.

Soubise (onion) sauce

2 large onions (sliced)
1 oz butter
½ pint white, or béchamel, sauce
  (use 1 oz butter to 2 tablespoons
  flour for roux)
1 tablespoon cream (optional)
salt and pepper

Serve with eggs and white meat (veal or rabbit).

Method

Blanch onion slices by putting in cold water, bringing to the boil and draining. Then melt butter in pan, add onion and cook, covered, until tender but not coloured (a piece of buttered paper or foil pressed down on to onion slices helps prevent colouring). Remove from pan and rub through a nylon strainer or work to a purée in an electric blender.

Add purée to a hot white or béchamel sauce, stir in the cream (if using) and season sauce well.

Velouté sauce

¾ oz butter
1 rounded tablespoon flour
⅓ –½ pint stock
2½ fl oz top of milk
salt and pepper
squeeze of lemon juice

For liaison (optional)
1 egg yolk (lightly beaten)
2 tablespoons cream

This sauce is made with a blond roux, at which point liquid is added. This is well-flavoured stock (made from veal, chicken or fish bones, according to dish with which sauce is being served), or liquid in which food was simmered or poached.

Velouté sauces are a base for others, such as caper, mustard, parsley or poulette.

Method

Melt butter in a saucepan, stir in flour and cook for about 5 seconds (blond roux). When roux is colour of pale straw, draw pan aside and cool slightly before pouring on stock.

Blend, return to heat and stir until thick. Add top of milk, season and bring to boil. Cook 4–5 minutes when sauce should be a syrupy consistency. If using a liaison, prepare by mixing egg yolk and cream together and then stir into sauce. Add lemon juice. Remove pan from heat.
Watchpoint Be careful not to let sauce boil after liaison has been added, otherwise the mixture will curdle.

Caper sauce

1 rounded tablespoon capers
1 dessertspoon chopped parsley
½ pint velouté sauce

Serve with boiled mutton or rabbit.

Method

Make velouté sauce. Then stir in the capers and parsley.

Mustard sauce

1 teaspoon made mustard (French, or English)
½ pint velouté sauce

Serve with boiled fish, grilled herrings and mackerel.

Method

Make velouté sauce. Mix mustard with 1 tablespoon of sauce, then stir into sauce.

Parsley sauce

1 large handful of fresh parsley (picked from stalks)
½ pint velouté sauce

Serve with eggs, fish or boiled chicken.

Method

Make velouté sauce. Wash parsley sprigs, boil for 7 minutes in pan of salted water; drain, press out moisture, then rub through a wire strainer. Beat into hot velouté sauce.

Or add cooked drained parsley to half the sauce without sieving and work in an electric blender.

Poulette sauce

½ pint velouté sauce
1 rounded teaspoon finely chopped
    parsley
1 teaspoon lemon juice
pinch of savory (chopped)

For liaison
1 egg yolk
2 tablespoons cream

Serve with carrots, broad beans, new potatoes, or boiled veal. Half this quantity is enough for dish of vegetables for 4–6 people.

Method

Add all ingredients, except the liaison, to velouté sauce. Mix thoroughly and boil. Make liaison by working egg yolk and cream together, add 1 tablespoon of hot sauce, then return this slowly to sauce; reheat carefully but do not reboil.

How to make brown sauces

A brown sauce for everyday use can be made from household stock or even a bouillon cube, and is suitable for serving with cutlets, rissoles and similar dishes. But a brown sauce, which is known as a 'sauce mère' (a parent sauce from which others are derived as with a béchamel or velouté sauce), is in the category of advanced cookery.

From the basic parent sauce, demi-glace (half-glaze), a number of advanced sauces can be made.

When the famous French chef Carême (who was once chief cook to the Prince Regent, later King George IV) made his demi-espagnole sauce—which today would be called demi-glace—he described it as 'gradually taking on that brilliant glaze which delights the eye when it first appears . . .'

General points

Every detail must be right for a perfect sauce and as this does call for a little time and trouble, it is sensible to double or treble the quantities and store the excess sauce in a covered container in the refrigerator, where it will keep for a week.

Much depends on the stock with which the sauce is made. It should be a clear brown bone stock, free of grease and set to a light, but not too firm, jelly. This will give a good flavour and a fine glossy texture to the sauce.

Do not add more flour than the recipe gives. The consistency of the finished sauce should be that of single cream.

How to make brown sauces continued

This 'half-glaze' is achieved by reduction of the bone stock in the sauce rather than by the addition of extra flour (which is used in the first instance merely to absorb the fat and bind the ingredients together).

Note: all these recipes will make $\frac{1}{2}$ pint quantity of sauce. 1 rounded tablespoon, ie. as much above as below the rim, is equivalent to $\frac{1}{2}$ oz sifted flour; 1 level tablespoon equals $\frac{1}{4}$ oz sifted flour.

Basic brown (demi-glace) sauce

3 tablespoons salad oil
1 small onion (finely diced)
1 small carrot (finely diced)
½ stick of celery (finely diced)
1 rounded tablespoon flour
1 teaspoon tomato purée
1 tablespoon chopped mushroom peelings, or 1 mushroom
1 pint well-flavoured brown bone stock
bouquet garni
salt and pepper

Method

Heat a saucepan, put in the oil and then add diced vegetables (of which there should be no more than 3 tablespoons in all). Lower heat and cook gently until vegetables are on point of changing colour; an indication of this is when they shrink slightly.

Mix in the flour and brown it slowly, stirring occasionally with a metal spoon and scraping the flour well from the bottom of the pan. When it is a good colour draw pan aside, cool a little, add tomato purée and chopped peelings or mushroom, ¾ pint of cold stock, bouquet garni and seasoning.

Bring to the boil, partially cover pan and cook gently for about 35-40 minutes. Skim off any scum which rises to the surface during this time. Add half the reserved stock, bring again to boil and skim. Simmer for 5 minutes. Add rest of stock, bring to boil and skim again.

Watchpoint Addition of cold stock accelerates rising of scum and so helps to clear the sauce.

Cook for a further 5 minutes, then strain, pressing vegetables gently to extract the juice. Rinse out the pan and return sauce to it. Partially cover and continue to cook gently until syrupy in consistency. It is now ready to be used on its own or as a base for any of the following sauces.

When serving a grill, 1-2 teaspoons of this sauce, added to a gravy or mixed with the juices in the grill pan, makes a great improvement.

Sauce espagnole

2 oz mushrooms (chopped)
1 rounded tablespoon tomato purée
$\frac{3}{4}$ pint demi-glace sauce
$\frac{1}{2}$ gill ($\frac{1}{8}$ pint) jellied stock
$\frac{1}{2}$ gill brown sherry
$\frac{1}{2}$ oz butter

Serve with dark meats.

Method

Put mushrooms in tomato purée and add both to prepared demi-glace sauce in a pan. Simmer for 5 minutes, then add stock. Continue to simmer, skimming often, until well reduced, then add sherry and beat in butter. Do not boil after this but keep warm in a bain marie or reheat when necessary.

Sauce madère

1 rounded tablespoon tomato purée
$\frac{3}{4}$ pint demi-glace sauce
$\frac{1}{2}$ gill ($\frac{1}{8}$ pint) jellied stock
$\frac{1}{2}$ gill Madeira wine
$\frac{1}{2}$ oz butter

Serve with roast/braised fillet, cutlets, escalopes, or chicken.

Method

Add tomato purée to the prepared demi-glace sauce and simmer for 5 minutes, then add stock. Continue to simmer, skimming often, until well reduced. Then add wine and beat in butter. Do not boil after this, but keep warm in a bain marie or reheat when necessary.

Sauce bigarade

1 shallot (finely chopped)
$\frac{1}{2}$ oz butter
$1\frac{1}{2}$ wineglasses red wine (Burgundy)
1 small bayleaf
1 Seville orange
$\frac{1}{2}$ pint demi-glace sauce
2 teaspoons redcurrant jelly
squeeze of lemon juice

Serve with duck, venison, pork.

Method

Put the shallot and butter into a small pan, cover and cook gently for 1 minute. Add wine, bayleaf and pared rind of $\frac{1}{2}$ orange. Simmer to reduce by about one-quarter. Strain into prepared demi-glace sauce, add redcurrant jelly and dissolve over a low heat.

Pare and cut rest of orange rind into needle-like shreds. Blanch in boiling water for 5 minutes, then drain. Add to sauce. Cut skin and pith from orange, cut out segments. Squeeze the white membranes to extract any juice for adding to the sauce with the lemon juice. Simmer for 4-5 minutes, then add orange segments. Reheat but do not boil.

Bigarade is the French name for a Seville orange; a sweet orange can replace it with extra lemon juice for sharpness; instead of the segments of sweet orange, juice of $\frac{1}{2}$ an orange can be substituted.

Sauce chasseur

1 shallot (finely chopped)
½ oz butter
2 oz button mushrooms (sliced)
1 large wineglass white wine
1 dessertspoon tomato purée
½ pint demi-glace sauce

Serve with all meats and with chicken, grilled or roasted.

Method

Cook shallot in butter in a pan for 1 minute, add mushrooms and cook for 2 minutes before adding wine. Simmer to reduce by one-third then add, with tomato purée, to prepared demi-glace sauce. Simmer for 3-4 minutes before using.

Sauce bordelaise

2 shallots (finely chopped)
2 wineglasses Bordeaux (Claret)
1 small sprig of thyme
¼ bayleaf
¾ pint demi-glace sauce (preferably made with veal bone stock)
little extra veal bone stock
1 teaspoon arrowroot (mixed with 1 tablespoon stock)
1–2 marrow bones, or ¾ oz butter

Serve with beef roasts or grills.

Method

Put shallots, wine and herbs into a pan, simmer to reduce by about one-third, then add to prepared demi-glace sauce. Bring to boil and simmer for 6-7 minutes, skimming well. Add a dash of cold stock to help skimming. When you have a good, concentrated flavour, thicken, if necessary, with arrowroot. Strain into a clean pan and keep warm.

With a knife dipped in hot water, scoop marrow from marrow bone and cut into small dice. Poach for 6-7 minutes in water just on boil. Drain carefully on a piece of muslin or absorbent paper. Add to sauce just before serving.

If not using marrow bones, briskly stir in butter in small pieces just before serving.

Bordelaise applies to many different dishes, the characteristics of the sauce being red or white wine and marrow bone fat.

How to make butter sauces

These are basic (mère) sauces from which others are derived. They usually form an accompaniment to fish, vegetables and meat, and should always be served lukewarm.

The best known are **hollandaise** and **béarnaise**. A small quantity of hollandaise is often added to a velouté or béchamel sauce for coating fish or delicate meats such as veal or chicken.

It is worth making a good quantity of hollandaise at a time as it can be kept in a screw-top container in the refrigerator. If using hollandaise in another sauce, or making it to keep, omit the cream in the recipe given overleaf.

Béarnaise sauce is based on hollandaise but is sharper and finished with herbs. To get the sharpness the vinegar is not reduced as much as for hollandaise sauce. It is the classic accompaniment to fillet steaks and tournedos.

Sauce blanche au beurre (white sauce with butter) is a useful one and may be served with white meats, veal or chicken. It is an excellent base for a caper sauce, and with the addition of 1-2 egg yolks becomes 'mock hollandaise' (sauce bâtarde), which is more economical and easier to handle than true hollandaise.

Sauce blanche au beurre

2 oz butter
1 tablespoon flour
$\frac{1}{2}$ pint water (boiling)
salt and pepper
good squeeze of lemon juice

Method

Melt a good $\frac{1}{2}$ oz of butter in a pan, stir in the flour off the heat and when smooth pour on all the boiling water, stirring or whisking briskly all the time.

Now add remaining butter in small pieces, stirring it well in. Season and add lemon juice.

Watchpoint If the water is really boiling it will cook flour. On no account bring sauce to the boil as this will give it an unpleasant gluey taste.

Sauce bâtarde (mock hollandaise)

Make the same basic sauce and add 1-2 egg yolks after the boiling water. Then add the remaining butter, seasoning and lemon juice.

Caper sauce

Make the same basic sauce and add 2 tablespoons coarsely chopped capers and 1 dessertspoon chopped parsley to the completed sauce.

Caper sauce can have an egg yolk added, if wished.

Hollandaise sauce

4 tablespoons white wine vinegar
6 peppercorns
1 blade mace
1 slice of onion
1 small bayleaf
3 egg yolks
5 oz butter (unsalted)
salt and pepper
1–2 tablespoons single cream, or
   top of milk
squeeze of lemon juice (optional)

Method

Put the vinegar into a small pan with the spices, onion and bayleaf. Boil this until reduced to a scant tablespoon, then set aside.

Cream egg yolks in a bowl with a good nut of butter and a pinch of salt. Strain on the vinegar mixture, set the bowl on a pan of boiling water, turn off heat and add remaining butter in small pieces, stirring vigorously all the time.

Watchpoint When adding butter, it should be slightly soft, not straight from refrigerator.

When all the butter has been added and the sauce is thick, taste for seasoning and add the cream or milk and lemon juice. The sauce should be pleasantly sharp yet bland, and should have consistency of thick cream.

Mousseline sauce

2 egg yolks
3 oz butter (unsalted)
juice of $\frac{1}{2}$ lemon
4 tablespoons double cream (lightly whipped)
salt and pepper

Serve separately with asparagus, lamb cutlets and salmon. It is lighter, fluffier and more delicate than a hollandaise.

Method

Put the yolks into a bowl, add a nut of butter and stand bowl in a bain marie (see page 62). Work until mixture is thick, then add lemon juice and season lightly. Whisk over the bain marie, add the remaining butter (slightly softened) by degrees.

When sauce is thick remove from heat and continue to whisk for 1-2 minutes. Then fold in the cream, adjust seasoning and serve.

True meat glaze is made from strained brown bone stock (see page 67), boiled down until it is thick, syrupy and brown in colour, which will take some time (a drop or two of gravy browning can be added to help this). Cool a little before use.

Béarnaise sauce

3 tablespoons wine vinegar
6 peppercorns
$\frac{1}{2}$ bayleaf
1 blade of mace
1 slice of onion
2 egg yolks
salt and pepper
3–4 oz butter (unsalted), softened
nut of meat glaze, or jelly at base of cake of beef dripping
1 teaspoon chopped mixed herbs (tarragon, chervil, and parsley)
pinch of snipped chives, or grated onion

This quantity is sufficient to put on steaks or cutlets but ingredients should be increased in proportion for a sauce to be served separately.

Method

Put the vinegar, peppercorns, bayleaf, mace and slice of onion into a small pan and boil until reduced to 1 tablespoon. Set pan aside.

Place the yolks in a small basin and beat well with a pinch of salt and a nut of butter. Strain on vinegar mixture and set the bowl on a pan of boiling water. Turn off heat and stir until beginning to thicken.

Add the softened butter in small pieces, each about the size of a hazelnut, stirring all the time. Season with pepper. Add the meat glaze, herbs, and chives or grated onion. Keep warm and use as required.

The finished sauce should have consistency of whipped cream.

Genevoise sauce

$2\frac{1}{2}$ oz butter
1 tablespoon flour
$\frac{1}{2}$ pint court bouillon (from fish it's
    being served with), or light stock
2 egg yolks
1–2 tablespoons cream, or top of
    milk
2–3 fillets anchovy (soaked in milk)
    – optional
1 heaped teaspoon anchovy essence
pepper
1 dessertspoon chopped parsley

Serve separately with poached
or grilled fish.

Method

Melt about $\frac{3}{4}$ oz of butter in a
pan, stir in flour and pour on
court bouillon or stock. Blend
and stir until boiling. Leave to
simmer for 2-3 minutes.

    Meanwhile mix egg yolks and
cream together in a basin;
drain and crush anchovies
thoroughly with the essence
(fillets can be omitted and a
little more essence used).

    Draw sauce aside and pour a
little on to yolk mixture, stirring
well, then return by degrees to
pan. Beat in remaining butter in
small pieces with anchovies,
add pepper to taste and parsley.
Reheat carefully but do not boil.

Ravigote sauce

1 shallot (finely chopped)
2–3 tablespoons wine vinegar
$\frac{1}{2}$ oz butter
$\frac{1}{2}$ pint sauce bâtarde (mock
    hollandaise)
1 scant teaspoon French mustard
1 tablespoon chopped mixed herbs
    (tarragon, chives and parsley)

Serve with grilled pork chops,
salmon and fried fish.

Method

    Simmer shallot in a pan in the
wine vinegar with the butter
until tender (2-3 minutes). Add
to the prepared sauce bâtarde
with the mustard and herbs.
Reheat gently.

    This sauce should be slightly
sharp and well flavoured with
the herbs.

Meat management

Beef

Choice of cuts

A mixture of the best and the cheaper cuts is often a good investment, eg. a piece of **skirt** or **chuck** bought with the tail end of the **sirloin**. As both skirt and chuck have little, if any, fat the tail end gives additional richness. Alternatively, the tail or thin end could be salted, and then cooked gently with onions, carrots and dumplings to make a lunch dish. Or the meat could be steamed for about 2 hours until tender, then pressed and used cold.

A good **frying steak,** or mock fillet, can be made from the 'nut' of meat that lies along the **blade bone.** Ask your butcher to cut this for you; and then, if you decide to roast it whole, either lard or bard it with pork fat, or wrap it in beef fat.

Alternatively it could be sliced, batted out well and cooked as steak 'à la minute'. Keep it underdone, as it is more tender like that, and pour over noisette butter at the last minute to keep it succulent.

The more coarsely grained and fibrous meat, eg, **top ribs** (Jacob's ladder), **aitchbone** and **topside,** are all better roasted underdone, the latter two being specially suited to spit roasting.

If using top ribs, roast two-thirds to serve hot first, and then cold. Turn the remaining third into a hot pot with kidney, covered by a layer of sliced potatoes which will absorb the fat from the ribs and make a crisp and succulent topping.

Wing rib, which is the start of the hind quarter, is bought according to the number of ribs required, ie. a 1 bone joint is about 3 lb.

Rib roasts (known as **rolled ribs** if taken off the bone) are 4-5 lb upwards. Cut off about half this, fill with a herb stuffing and roast. The other half can be made into a pie or pudding with $\frac{1}{2}$ lb ox kidney.

A 5-6 lb piece of **sirloin,** with the **undercut,** is also an economical buy. The undercut can be removed and used for tournedos, steaks or for a small roast, the meat marbled with fat can be used with a piece of skirt as suggested previously and the top part can be roasted on the bone. This bone can be used to make stock when the joint has been eaten.

Carving beef

Sirloin

To make carving easier, see that the chine bone is sawn through before roasting. This will mean that the full length of the knife can be used without coming in contact with the bone. If at all possible, cut off the chine bone completely before starting to carve.

To carve sirloin with an undercut (or fillet), see the captions and photographs opposite. Give the outside slice to the person who prefers meat well done, together with a slice of the undercut taken from the outside edge.

For sirloin without an undercut, just slice the meat thinly.

1 *To carve sirloin with an under-cut, turn the joint upside-down on the dish, ie. on its back. If the butcher has sawn through the chine bone, remove this before starting*

3 *Turn the joint over and slice as thinly as possible down the whole length of the sirloin. Serve each person with a slice of undercut and a slice or two of the top part. Spoon over some of the gravy*

Wing rib

Carve as for sirloin without the undercut.

Fillet

Carve in $\frac{1}{4}$-inch thick slices down to the bone, in the same way as for the undercut on sirloin.

Rounds of beef

Set the meat on the carving dish with the cut sides top and bottom. Insert the fork, with the guard up, into the side of the joint to hold it steady.

Holding the knife horizontally, or slightly slanting, slice thinly from the top right across the grain of the meat.

2 *Slice downwards through the undercut to the bone, taking slices not less than $\frac{1}{4}$ inch thick for each person. Continue to carve towards the bone, and as you reach it loosen the meat around it*

Beef

English cuts

1 Neck (stew)
2 Top ribs (braise)
3 Rib roast (roast or braise)
4 Wing ribs (roast)
5 Sirloin (roast, or grill as steaks)
6 Rump (grill)
7 Aitchbone (roast or braise)
8 Topside and silverside (roast or braise)
9 Buttock and silverside (boil fresh or salted)
10 Shin and cow heel (stew)
11 Thick flank (stew, braise, boil or press)
12 Thin flank (stew, braise, boil or press)
13 Brisket (boil fresh or salted, or can be pressed)
14 Chuck steak (stew or braise)
15 Shin (stew, gravy or beef tea)
16 Sticking piece (stew)
17 Clod (stew)

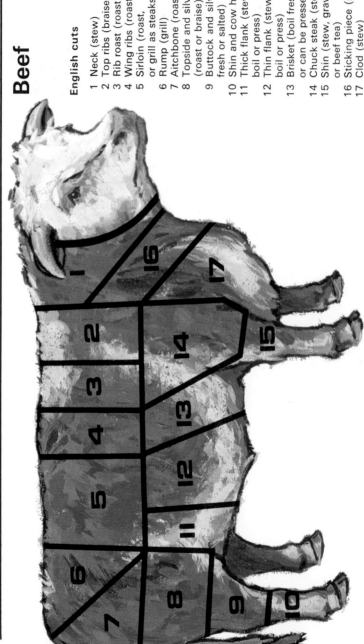

Beef

Scottish cuts

A Neck, or sticking piece (stew)
B Fore-knap bone (stew, gravy or beef tea)
C Fore-hough (stew, gravy or beef tea)
D Gullet (stew)
E Brisket (boil fresh or salted, or stew)
F Thick runner (stew or braise)
G Thin runner (stew or braise)
H Shoulder (braise)
I Flank (stew, braise, boil or press)
J Flank — top ribs (roast or boil)
K Flank — face of (stew, braise, boil or press)
L Rib roast (roast)
M Sirloin roast (roast)
N Pope's eye (roast or braise)
O Rump (roast, braise, or grill as steaks)
P Hind-hough (braise, or boil fresh or salted)
Q Hind-knap bone (stew)

Lamb and mutton

Choice of cuts

A joint which gives a variety of dishes is the **fore-quarter.** This consists of the **scrag, middle** and **best end of neck,** and the **shoulder** which may be cut off and roasted. Or, if this is too large a cut, just buy the whole neck. In both cases, the scrag and middle can be used for Irish stew or Scotch broth, or navarin, and the best end for cutlets or a roast.

Another useful cut is a whole **leg** or **gigot.** Choose one weighing 5-6 lb and divide it into three: fillet or top end, middle cut and knuckle. Roast the fillet end — this may be boned and rolled to make a small joint, and the bone used to make a broth with vegetables. The middle cut can form a sauté, and the knuckle can be pot roasted with tomatoes and onions.

English cuts

1 Head (broths)
2 Scrag (stew)
3 Shoulder (roast or braise)
4 Neck — best end, nearest loin
   (roast whole or grill as cutlets)

   — middle neck, nearest scrag
   (stew)
5 Loin, or saddle (roast or braise)
6 Leg (roast or braise)
7 Breast (stew or braise)

Carving lamb

Saddle

There are two ways of carving saddle. In the first, the slices are carved parallel to the backbone (see photographs 2 & 3 overleaf) ; in the second, which is the easier method if the joint is carved in the kitchen, the slices are cut diagonally or at right-angles to the bone.

For the second method, slide the knife down each side of the backbone (as in photograph 1), then slip it under the meat either side of the bone. Make a cut parallel to the bone about an inch above the dish, and then with the knife held at right-angles, or slightly diagonally to the bone cut the slices from the bone down the side to the cut line.

Then lift the slices back on to the bone, ready to be served in the dining room.

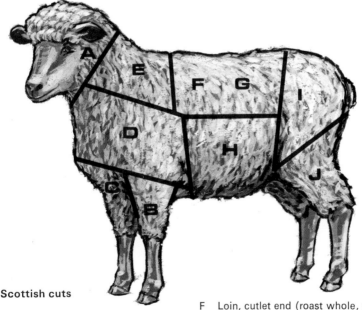

Scottish cuts

A   Neck (broths or stew)
B   Fore-shank (soups)
C   Breast (stew, braise or stuff and roast)
D   Shoulder, runner cuts (roast)
E   Shoulder, back rib cut (braise, boil or stew)
F   Loin, cutlet end (roast whole, or grill as cutlets)
G   Loin, double loin (roast)
H   Flank (roast or braise)
I   Gigot, chump end (roast, braise or boil)
J   Gigot, shank end (roast, braise or boil)

Lamb and mutton continued

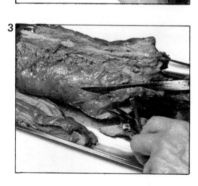

of the bone, cutting the pieces in half if the saddle is a large one
3 Cut slanting slices from the chump end of the saddle and then, for those who like a little fat, cut slanting slices from the crisp flap of the neck end

Shoulders and legs

Carve both these joints as shown in the photographs and captions 4-8.

To carve a shoulder successfully, it is necessary to know where the bone lies in relation to the meat, as this varies according to whether it is a left-hand or a right-hand shoulder (see the diagrams opposite).

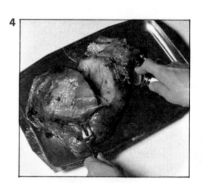

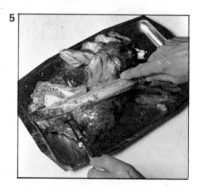

1 *Set the saddle on the carving dish with the tail end towards you. Run the knife down one side of the backbone, and then slip it under the meat which lies on the side of the bone. For more than 4 servings, repeat this on the other side of the bone*
2 *Carve 2–3 wedge-shaped slices down the whole length of each side*

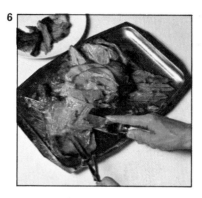

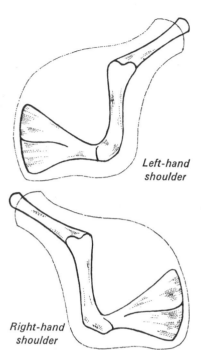

Left-hand shoulder

Right-hand shoulder

4 Set the shoulder on the serving dish with the meatiest side uppermost and the knuckle away from you (this may be either to the right — as here — or left, see diagrams). Tilt the joint slightly towards you and cut down to the bone in wedge-shaped pieces

5 With the fork, find the spine of the blade bone (the ridge along the top of the bone), and cut wedge-shaped slices lengthwise on either side

6 Turn the joint over and carve thinner pieces from the flat part of the blade bone

7 Set the leg on the carving dish with the round side uppermost and leaning away from you. Insert the fork near the knuckle and tilt the leg slightly towards you to raise it from the dish. Make the first cut diagonally down to the bone. This part has the sweetest meat. Then make another cut $\frac{1}{4}$-$\frac{1}{2}$ inch away to give a wedge-shaped slice

8 Continue to carve in this way towards the pelvic bone, slanting the knife as you progress. When this bone is reached, turn the joint over and slice thin pieces sideways and parallel to the leg bone

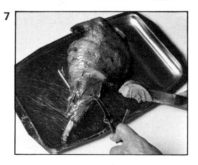

▶

Lamb and mutton continued

Best end of neck

To make something special of a best end, it is worthwhile learning how to prepare a carré d'agneau (see diagrams 1-6), and a crown roast (see diagrams 7-9).

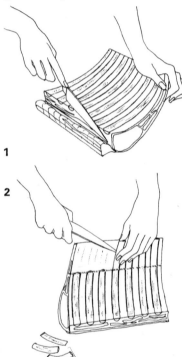

1

2

For a carré d'agneau, buy 1 best end of neck (weighing 2 lb) and ask the butcher to chine it and saw a line across the cutlet bones about 2½ inches long, starting from the noix (nut of meat).

1 Start preparing the joint by removing chine bone (use for gravy).
2 Place the joint with the noix furthest away from you. With a sharp knife, and working from the sawn line, cut out and remove the short ends of the cutlet bones

3 Cut and loosen the remaining cutlet bones to within ½ inch of the noix, but leave the bones attached
4 Make slits through the meat about 2½ inches long, starting from the sawn edge of the bones, by running the blade of the knife along the side of each cutlet bone. Then push the bones through

3

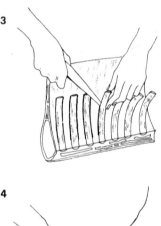

4

5

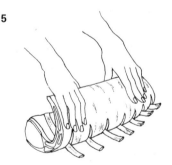

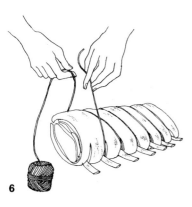

6

For a crown roast, buy 2 best ends of neck (each weighing 2 lb) and have them chined by the butcher. To prepare, first remove the chine bone.

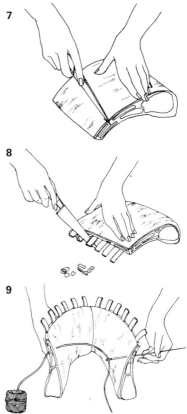

5 *Drawing the meat up and back towards the noix, press down firmly so that the fatty edges meet (as for a noisette) and the cutlet bones are fully exposed. Cut off a small part of long flat end if this overlaps the noix*

6 *Tie up the joint, bringing the string round the meat in the slits alongside each cutlet bone. To cook: roast as for best end (ie. 20 minutes per lb and 20 minutes over at 375°F or Mark 6 — oven settings are not exactly comparable). Carve by slicing down alongside each bone*

7 *With a sharp knife, cut through the flesh an inch or so from the end of cutlet bones on each joint*

8 *Remove the fat and meat from both joints, scraping bones clean*

9 *Using fine string and a trussing needle, sew joints together, back to back (ie. with the fat inside), and with the bones curving outwards. Roast as for best end, basting frequently to ensure the fat is good and crisp*

Pork

Choice of cuts

Gammon is usually the fore leg of pig which has been 'wet cured', ie. in a brine solution. Like bacon (the pig's side which is cured with the leg), gammon may be smoked or unsmoked (green). Ham comes from the hind leg (as can gammon), and is 'dry cured' in a mixture of salt and saltpetre.

A useful pork joint to buy is the **hand and shoulder.** When boned this can weigh about 11 lb or even more, so if this is too much, even for your home freezer, ask the butcher to cut the weight you want.

Use the blade bone end for roasting. Salt the remainder and boil it to serve with pease pudding. Alternatively make it into brawn, augmented by $\frac{1}{2}$ lb shin of beef, if wished.

Buy **gammon** weighing 3-4 lb and braise whole and serve hot with a spinach purée; or boil, then glaze with sugar in the oven, and serve cold.

Alternatively cut off a third and mince it and mix with about 1 lb minced beef or veal to make a meat loaf to serve hot or cold.

Carving pork

When carving the loin or a piece of the leg with crackling (only these joints have crackling), slice it away first. It can be cut into pieces and put on the dish ready to serve.

Loin should be chined to make carving easier, and leg should be carved in moderately thin slices down to the bone.

Carving ham

Carving a ham in the kitchen is usually done as follows:

Set the ham on the dish or board with the rounded side of the joint away from you as for lamb. Make a cut about 3 inches from the shank bone, first inserting the fork on the near side of the bone right down to the dish or board.

continued on page 98

Shoulder of ham, carved down to the bone in wedge-shaped slices

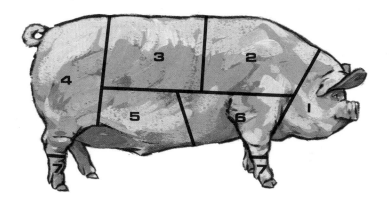

English cuts

1 Head (brawn)
2 Neck, or fore loin (roast or braise)
3 Loin (roast, or grill/fry as chops)
4 Leg (roast or boil)

5 Belly and spring (boil fresh or salted)
6 Hand (roast or boil)
7 Trotters (boil or braise)

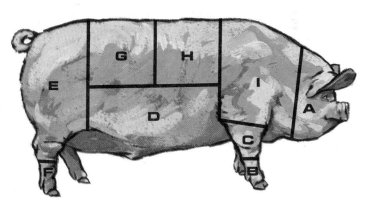

Scottish cuts

A   Head (brawn)
B   F Trotter (boil or braise)
C   Fore-hough (stock)
D   Flank (boil fresh or salted)
E   Gigot (roast)

G   Loin, double loin (roast, or grill/fry as chops)
H   Loin, cutlet (roast, or grill/fry as chops)
I   Shoulder (roast or braise)

Pork continued

Slice the ham in wedge-shaped slices a little less than $\frac{1}{4}$-inch thick, taking the knife right down to the bone and removing the slices as you go.

Continue to slice thinly down to the bone, and after the first 12 or so slices, begin to slant the knife so that when the top bone is reached the knife is almost flat as you carve.

To make the joint tidy again, make sure that the knife goes right down to the bone, and slice off the odd pieces that lie on the far side of the bone.

Carving a ham by the method used in shops and delicatessens involves the use of a ham stand and a ham knife.

The ham is sliced longways, and cut with the grain instead of transversely, as in the first method. Start carving on the rounded side, and allow the knife to travel from the top bone down to the shank, cutting as thin slices as possible.

Carving Turkey

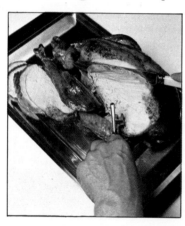

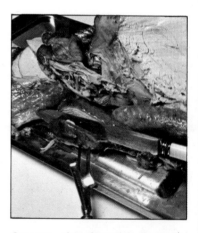

Set the bird on the carving dish with the breast towards you. Insert the fork into the carcass between the leg and the breast, then slice the skin between the leg and carcass and bend the leg outwards. Carve the breast in curving slices, starting from the wing and working up to the rib-cage (as shown), and taking in a piece of breast stuffing

Separate the drumstick from the thigh joint and then cut thin slices of dark meat from these. Serve each person with a portion of this, a slice of breast and some stuffing. When you have completed one side of the bird, turn it round and carve the other side in the same way

Roasting

Roasting is the traditional – and most popular – method of cooking in this country, so it is up to every serious student of cookery to master this most important art.

True roasting was always done on a revolving spit over an open fire. Only recently, however, has this become a practical reality in the home. Gas-fired and electric spits are now combined with the grill on many domestic cookers, or can be bought as separate units.

If you are not lucky enough to own a spit, you can obtain equally good results by roasting the meat in the oven. But extra care is needed because cooking in the oven is really baking. For the best results, follow these hints.

Remove the meat from the refrigerator 30 minutes before cooking – all meat for roasting should be at room temperature.

Pre-heat the oven to the correct temperature, first checking that the shelf is in position and will take the joint comfortably. The correct position varies with the type of oven, so follow the manufacturer's instructions carefully.

Put the roasting tin in the oven with 2–3 tablespoons of dripping, depending on the size of the joint.

When the dripping is smoking, set the meat on a grid or simply on the bottom of the tin. Baste well to seal in the juices and return to the oven. If you are not using a grid, place the joint on its edge rather than flat on the outside, since the part in contact with the tin may get hard and overcook. This is especially important with a round joint, eg. sirloin.

Cook according to the weight and thickness of the joint (see chart, page 102), basting every 15–20 minutes to keep the meat moist and tender until done.

Once the meat is cooked, it should be dished up and placed in the warming drawer of the cooker. Plan the cooking time to allow the meat to stand for 15 minutes while the gravy is prepared and vegetables dished up. This standing time will make the meat much easier to carve.

A roast joint needs good gravy: strong and clear for beef, mutton and lamb, and lightly-thickened for pork and veal. Serve gravy separately in a gravy boat.

99

Beef cuts for roasting

When beef is well hung, as it should be, it is purplish-red in colour. Beef that is too fresh and bright red improves if kept in refrigerator for a few days before cooking. Fat should be creamy in colour. In prime cuts, like sirloin, there is a light marbling of fat through lean meat. Fat helps to keep a joint tender, so make sure its natural fat is adhering and not an extra slab which has been tied on by the butcher. Accompaniments for roast beef are given on pages 103 and 104. For roasting times, see page 102 and page 113 for slow and spit roasting.

Sirloin

The joint should weigh not less than $3\frac{1}{2}$-4 lb on the bone and contain the undercut or fillet. It can be boned and rolled, although meat is juicier and has more flavour when roasted on the bone. Butchers often bone and roll sirloin in order to make smaller joints from this prime cut. Continental butchers offer contrefilet, or entrecôte, a compact joint from the top of the sirloin. It is always well trimmed, free of bone and excess fat, so it is expensive.

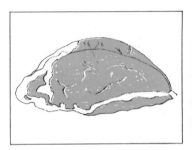

Fillet

An excellent joint for a party or the cold table, fillet is the undercut from the sirloin which can extend into the rump (rump fillet). It has little or no fat and so is frequently larded (ie. wrapped round with pork fat, or larding bacon, which can, alternatively, be sewn in the surface of the joint with a larding needle).

Since fillet is a small joint of 2 lb and upwards, it must have a fierce oven and be roasted on a grid. It is very tender meat.

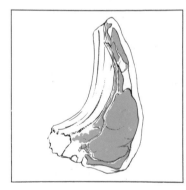

Rib roast and wing rib

Large joints of 4-5 lb and upwards. Like sirloin, these can be boned and rolled.

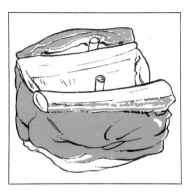

Tops ribs,
or
Jacob's ladder

This joint is called Jacob's ladder because the lean meat and fat layers on top of the bone make it rise during cooking and so resemble the rungs of a ladder. If you like fat, you will like Jacob's ladder, and this joint is excellent eaten cold.

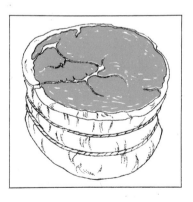

Topside

Although sold as a roasting joint, topside is really better braised or pot roasted. If roasted, it must be left rare or underdone to keep it tender because the meat is exceptionally lean. Overcooking makes this cut dry and hard. Small joints of $1\frac{1}{2}$ lb and upwards can be cut from topside.

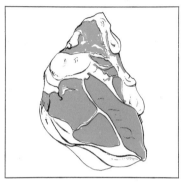

Aitchbone

This is a very large joint rarely cut these days, lying between the rump, topside and silverside. On the bone (pelvic) it weighs about 12 lb, but nowadays butchers usually remove the bone and cut roughly triangular shaped joints from this section that weigh $2\frac{1}{2}$-$4\frac{1}{2}$ lb. The meat has a good flavour and is tender. At the apex it is fine-grained with natural fat adhering. At the base the meat is lean and rather coarse-grained, so it is better under-roasted.

Roasting times for meat

	Oven temperature	Total cooking time (equal for gas and electricity)
Beef	Electric oven 375°F Gas Mark 7 for the first 15 minutes, then reduce to Mark 6	Rare: 15 minutes per lb and 15 minutes over Well done: 20 minutes per lb and 30 minutes over Since the cooking time varies with the thickness of the joint and not always according to the weight, allow: 45 minutes for joints under $1\frac{1}{2}$ lb $1\frac{1}{4}$ hours for joints under 3 lb
Lamb	Electric oven 375°F Gas Mark 6	20 minutes per lb and 20 minutes over
Mutton	Electric oven 375°F Gas Mark 6 for the first 15 minutes, then reduce to Mark 5	20 minutes per lb and 20 minutes over
Pork	Electric oven 375°F Gas Mark 7 for the first 15 minutes, then reduce to Mark 6	25 minutes per lb and 25 minutes over

The electricity settings and gas Marks given here are not always comparable because an electric oven, being entirely enclosed, gives a constant heat all over, whereas a gas oven, with its open flue, has 3 different heat zones.

Accompaniments to beef roasts

Yorkshire pudding

5 oz plain flour
pinch of salt
1 large egg
½ pint milk and water mixed (¾ milk
   to ¼ water)
1 tablespoon dripping
1 tablespoon beef suet (finely
   grated) – optional

Method

Sift the flour with the salt into a
mixing bowl. Make a well in the
centre and put in the unbeaten
egg and half the milk and water.
Stir carefully, gradually drawing
in the flour. Add half the remaining milk and water and
beat well. Stir in the rest of the
liquid and leave in a cool place
for about 1 hour before cooking.
   Set the oven at 400-450°F or
Mark 7.
   Heat the dripping in a shallow
dish until hot (a tin or enamel
dish is most satisfactory). Tilt
the dish round to coat sides with
the hot dripping. Then pour in
the batter. Bake for 30-40 minutes in the pre-set hot oven on a
shelf well above the meat.
   This recipe gives a light, well-
risen pudding. If you prefer
something more substantial,
stir 1 tablespoon beef suet
(finely grated) into the mixture
before baking.

Horseradish cream

2 tablespoons freshly grated
   horseradish
1 dessertspoon white wine
   vinegar
1 teaspoon dry mustard
1 rounded teaspoon caster sugar
pinch of salt
black pepper (ground from mill)
1 small carton (2½ fl oz) double
   cream

Method

Mix the vinegar and seasonings
together and add the horseradish. Lightly whip the cream
and mix gently into the other
ingredients.
   When fresh horseradish is
unobtainable, use grated horseradish preserved in vinegar and
mix the seasoning with only
1 teaspoon of vinegar.

Gravy

The basis of gravy is, of course, the meat's sediment and juices left in the roasting tin. To increase the amount, add stock. For mutton and lamb, simmer the knuckle bone from the leg or shoulder (or the chine bone from the loin) with water and vegetables to flavour. For a joint of beef, when no bone or stock is available, potato water or a bouillon cube can be used, but be sparing with seasoning since both can be salty.

When the meat is dished up, tilt the roasting tin gently to pour off the fat, but keep back the juices and sediment from the meat. Dust in just enough flour to absorb the small quantity of dripping left in the roasting tin (not usually more than 1 dessertspoon of flour for beef or lamb). Allow to colour very slowly, then scrape tin well to take up the sediment round the sides.

Pour on $\frac{1}{2}$-$\frac{3}{4}$ pint stock, bring to the boil and season with salt and pepper. Reduce the quantity to concentrate the flavour. If necessary, you can improve the colour with a little gravy browning. This is better than scorching the flour in a thin roasting tin. Strain into a gravy boat. Serve very hot.

There's nothing quite like a tender joint of roast beef, slightly pink in the centre, with baked (roast) potatoes and Yorkshire pudding

Lamb cuts for roasting

The size of the carcass varies with the breed of lamb, but the best is small with a reasonable covering of firm white fat. The meat is pale to dark red in colour. As with beef, lamb tastes better if it has been hung. It should not be served underdone, but should have just a tinge of pink at the centre. Mint sauce is traditionally served with lamb. Other accompaniments are given on page 108. For roasting times see pages 102 and 113.

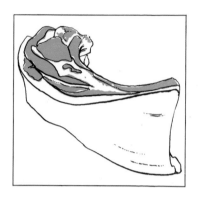

Crown roast

Ask your butcher to prepare this joint, which is good for dinner parties of 6-8 people. Its crown shape is achieved by turning outwards two best ends of neck, which are then trussed and skewered together to form a circle. The centre of this roast may be stuffed or filled with spring vegetables before serving. Crown the top bones with cutlet frills.

Best end of neck

An excellent small joint for 3-4 people, the whole best end consists of 6-7 cutlet bones and weighs $1\frac{1}{2}$-2 lb. The joint should be chined and the bones sawn through 2-3 inches from the top.

To prepare neck for roasting: first, cut away the chine bone (half backbone) and keep for making gravy. Then cut off the flap containing the top of the cutlet bones and keep for roasting with the neck — but cut into pieces before serving. The fat from the top of the bones should be sliced away to a depth of $1\frac{1}{2}$-2 inches. Cut away gristly meat between the cleared bones with a small knife and scrape bone clean. Be sure to skin the fat side of the neck (if not already done by the butcher) and score in a lattice pattern with the point of the knife.

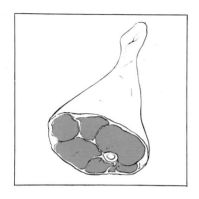

Leg

This is the leanest cut so it needs to be well basted during roasting. The weight varies from 3-5 lb, and the largest legs are frequently halved and sold as shank and fillet end.

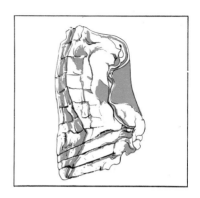

Loin

Loin is very sweet meat. It is rather wasteful because of a generous amount of fat on the underside. Carving is easier if the joint is chined, not chopped, by the butcher. It is good when boned and stuffed.

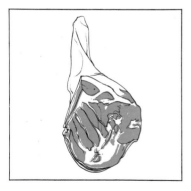

Shoulder

Particularly well flavoured and juicy, shoulder has a good proportion of fat to lean. It is equally good roasted plain, or boned and stuffed.

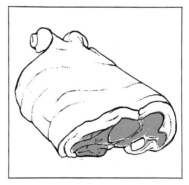

Saddle

The joint for a big party or special occasion, saddle is the double loin taken from the top end down to the tail and corresponds to a baron of beef. Its weight averages 8-10 lb and this will serve 8-10 people.

Accompaniments to lamb roasts

Mint sauce

2 tablespoons fresh mint
1–2 tablespoons caster sugar
1–2 tablespoons boiling water
wine vinegar (to taste)

Method

Mint sauce should be bright green, smooth and pulpy in consistency. Chop the mint and pound with the caster sugar until quite smooth. Add 1-2 tablespoons boiling water, according to the quantity of mint, to improve the colour and melt the sugar. Add a little wine vinegar to taste.

Onion sauce

3 medium-size onions
1 oz butter
2 tablespoons plain flour
$\frac{1}{2}$ pint milk, scalded
salt and pepper
1 tablespoon cream, or
  $\frac{1}{2}$ oz butter (optional)

Method

Slice the onions and cook in boiling salted water until tender. Drain thoroughly and sieve, or blend if you prefer a smooth sauce.

Melt the butter, take off the heat and add the flour. Tip on the scalded milk (scalding the milk will make it less likely to curdle) and, when thoroughly blended, stir continually over moderate heat until boiling. Simmer 2-3 minutes, add the prepared onions, adjust seasoning and finish with a spoonful of cream or a knob of butter.

Redcurrant jelly

It is not possible to give a specific quantity of redcurrants as the recipe is governed by the amount of juice made, which is variable.

Method

Wash the fruit and, without removing from the stems, put in a 7 lb jam jar or stone crock. Cover and stand in deep pan of hot water. Simmer on top of the stove or in the oven at 350°F or Mark 4, mashing the fruit a little from time to time, until all the juice is extracted (about 1 hour).

Then turn fruit into a jelly-bag, or double linen strainer, and allow to drain undisturbed overnight over a basin.

Watchpoint To keep the jelly clear and sparkling, do not try to speed up the draining process by forcing juice through; this will only make the jelly cloudy.

Now measure juice. Allowing 1 lb lump or preserving sugar to each pint of juice, mix juice and sugar together, dissolving over slow heat. When dissolved, bring to the boil, boil hard for 3-5 minutes and skim with a wooden spoon. Test a little on a saucer: allow jelly to cool, tilt saucer and, if jelly is set, it will wrinkle. Put into jam jars, place small circles of greaseproof paper over jelly, label and cover with jam pot covers. Store in a dry larder until required.

Pork cuts for roasting

The flesh of pork should be firm, the lean pinkish-white, and the fat white and smooth. The skin of the hindquarter gives the best crackling and both skin and rind should be thin and supple. Pork must always be well cooked to prevent the danger of infection which may be present in the meat. Any juices that run through the meat after cooking should be clear — not pink, which indicates undercooking. Roasting times are given on pages 102 and 113. For accompaniments see the following page.

Leg

A large joint weighing 10 lb or more. This is usually sold halved, knuckle or fillet end, or boned, rolled and cut into smaller joints. Make sure that the skin is well scored to give crisp crackling. A half leg can be boned and stuffed.

Loin

Loin is a joint that varies in size. It is cut from the top end down to the chump end. For easy carving, ask the butcher to chine the joint.

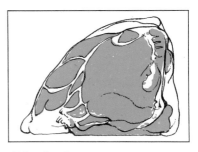

Blade bone or boned, rolled shoulder joints

Joints weighing 2-3½ lb, suitable for small family meals. The meat is sweet and tender but, since the joints are cut from the forequarter, do not expect the crackling to be crisp.

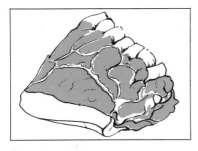

Spare rib

Good small joint for roasting or pot roasting.

Accompaniments to pork roasts

Apple sauce

1 lb cooking apples
rind of $\frac{1}{2}$ lemon
2–3 tablespoons water
1 dessertspoon caster sugar
$\frac{1}{2}$ oz butter

Method

Peel and core the apples. Pare the lemon rind thinly. Put apples and rind in a saucepan with 2-3 tablespoons water. Cover tightly and cook until pulpy. Beat with a wooden spoon until smooth, or put through a strainer. Stir in the sugar and butter. Serve hot.

Braised leeks

6 leeks
1 oz butter

Method

Trim the leeks, make a cross cut in the top and wash thoroughly under running water. Blanch by putting into boiling salted water for 1 minute. Drain well. Put in a well-buttered casserole, cover tightly and cook for 45-50 minutes on the bottom shelf of the oven at 325°F or Mark 3.

Sage and onion stuffing

3 medium-size onions
2 oz butter, or suet
6 oz fresh white breadcrumbs
2 teaspoons dried sage
1 teaspoon chopped parsley
salt and pepper
beaten egg, or milk

Method

Slice onions finely and boil 15—20 minutes in salted water. Drain and stir in the butter or suet. Add remaining ingredients, season well and mix with beaten egg or milk. If the joint is not suitable for stuffing, put the mixture into a small oven-proof dish, baste with 1 table-spoon of dripping and cook in the oven for 30-40 minutes at 400°F or Mark 6.

Slow and spit roasting

Through research into providing food at budget cost, it has been discovered that there is much less shrinkage if meat is slow roasted (the oven is set at 350°F or Mark 4 for pork, and at 325°F or Mark 3 for all other meats); and now that beef particularly is so expensive it is worthwhile for the housewife to experiment with this method and to benefit from the information obtained.

When slow roasting, the only way to ensure that the meat is fully cooked in the centre is to use a meat thermometer. The chart (see page 113) gives an approximate time per lb for the various joints of meat (assuming them to be at room temperature), and the temperatures your thermometer must register.

Remember the thermometer must be inserted into the thickest part of the meat and must never touch the bone, nor rest on the fat, and that the times given may vary with the size and shape of the joint, and also the amount of fat.

Joints on the bone must always be set on a rack, fat side uppermost, in the roasting tin. It is not necessary to add extra fat, nor is it necessary to baste. Boned and rolled joints, or those cut from boneless meat, should be spread with a little good dripping and set on a rack in the tin in the same way. There is no need to baste, but they should be turned half way through the cooking.

It is now possible for many more people to spit roast at home, and electrically operated rotating spits do give an almost exact copy of the old spit roast before an open fire. This method is more like slow roasting, the shrinkage is less, and the flavour is particularly fine as the outside fat develops such a good flavour. In fact, we feel that this is the only way to roast a joint of topside, a small lean joint which tends to become hard on the outside when oven-roasted.

It is important that meat to be spit roasted is at room temperature, so remove it from the refrigerator 30 minutes before cooking.

Joints with a cut surface are cooked on very high heat until the meat just begins to take colour. The heat should then be turned quite low (each cooker will have its own instructions in the handbook), and the meat is cooked at black heat (ie. not radiant heat) until it is tender. Follow the timing given in the chart (see page 113). Brush or baste the joint with dripping from time to time during the cooking.

Spit roasting guide
Beef
The cut surface of the joint must always be exposed to the heat in order to seal it and retain the juices. In a joint of wing rib or sirloin the spit should be inserted in such a position that it does not touch the bone, so that the fat and both sides of the lean of the meat are exposed in turn as the joint rotates. If the spit touches the bone it upsets the distribution of heat or may stop it altogether.

Lamb

A leg of lamb can be spit roasted but particular care must be taken in inserting the spit because of the position of the bone.

A shoulder of lamb should be fully or partially boned.

Pork

Joints cut from the leg should be boned and stuffed, but remember that the stuffing will swell, so it is wise to put in only the very minimum amount and secure it well by sewing up with a trussing needle and thread. Extra stuffing can always be made and cooked separately. Shoulder cuts, providing they have been removed from the bone, are suitable for spit roasting, but a whole leg would be too large.

Gravy for spit roasted joints

The making of a good gravy is something of a problem when spit roasting because although the drip tray will have collected a certain amount of juice and quite a lot of fat during the cooking time, the tin itself is not suitable for making gravy.

Any juices that fall from the meat, congeal and then brown on the drip tray must be carefully scooped up, added to a little good stock and then boiled up well. If the family likes plenty of gravy, this can be augmented by adding potato water, if there is no stock, and gravy salt for colouring and flavour. It can be thickened too, if liked.

SLOW ROASTING CHART

Set oven at 350°F or Mark 4 for pork,
and 325°F or Mark 3 for other meat

Cuts of meat	Minutes per lb for 3-6 lb joints	Temperature on meat thermometer
Beef on the bone		
sirloin — rare	26	140°F
wing rib — medium	30	160°F
rib roast — well done	35	170°F
Lamb		
leg	35-40	175°F-182°F
neck, best end and loin	45	182°F
shoulder	35	182°F
shoulder, boned and rolled	55	182°F
Pork		
leg	45-50	185°F
loin	35-40	185°F
shoulder, a joint from the blade	40-50	185°F
shoulder, boned and rolled	55	185°F
Veal		
leg	35-40	180°F
loin	35-40	180°F
shoulder, boneless roll	55	180°F

SPIT ROASTING CHART

	Minutes per lb
Beef	
without bone	10-25
with bone	20-25
Lamb	25-35
Pork	30-35
Hares and rabbits	
stuffed	20-25
unstuffed	15
Poultry	
stuffed	20-25
unstuffed	15-20

Sharpening Carving Knives

To sharpen carbon steel carving knives there is a technique. If using a steel, hold it slanting upwards in your left hand (if you are right-handed), and, holding the knife in your right hand, draw it rapidly up and down the steel with the knife slanting very slightly inwards. Avoid having too acute an angle or the cutting edge of the knife will have too direct a contact with the steel. To get an idea of the movement, watch your butcher sharpen his knife. Carbon steel kitchen knives can either be sharpened on a steel or on a fine carborundum. Dip the latter in water, and use the same movement as before for sharpening.

An alternative method, and perhaps one more suitable for those not fully experienced, is to draw the knife away from you 10-12 times up the carborundum. Then turn the knife over and draw it down towards you in the same way, always keeping the cutting edge away from you and the knife almost flat on the stone.

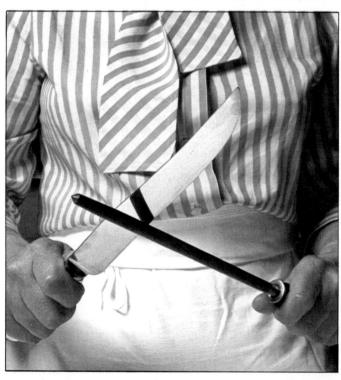

Stewing, casseroling and pot roasting

How to stew

Stewing means cooking food gently in liquid. The food can be meat of any kind, fish, vegetables or fruit.

In general, the meat used is not from the most expensive cuts, but from those that require long, slow cooking to make them tender and to bring out their flavour. Cuts with a slight marbling of fat or gristle are excellent stewed, and this marbling makes meat more succulent.

A stew can be either white or brown. In a white stew, sometimes called a fricassée, the meat is not browned but blanched to whiten and to take away strong flavours before cooking. The liquid is usually thickened after the meat has been cooked, or towards the end. A white stew is usually cooked on top of the stove.

In a brown stew, sometimes called a ragoût, meat is browned with or without vegetables and a little flour is stirred in just before the stock is added. It may be cooked either on top of the stove, or inside the oven which is easier.

Liquid in both brown and white stews must never be allowed to do more than simmer, since boiling will only toughen meat.

A stew may be an everyday dish, but it is easily turned into a party special by adding wine, cream or a garnish.

Preparation of stews

White stew. Soak meat well, preferably overnight, in plenty of cold salted water. Change the water once or twice during this process to take away any strong flavour. Then rinse and put into the pan ready for cooking; cover with fresh cold water, add salt and — for veal or rabbit — a slice of lemon to whiten meat. Blanch by bringing slowly to the boil, then skim, drain and refresh in cold water to wash away any scum. Return to the pan and add liquid specified in the recipe, usually just enough to cover meat.

Veal or chicken stock, not water, should be used, because it will make a much better sauce. Chicken does not need soaking unless it is jointed raw, and a boiling fowl should be blanched. Keep the pan covered.

Brown stew. Choose a thick, enamelled iron pan or flame-proof casserole, so that the stew can be cooked and served in it. Failing this, brown the meat in a frying pan and transfer it to a casserole, but make the sauce or gravy in the same frying pan to avoid losing any flavour.

Cut meat (without bone) into 2-inch squares, leaving on a small amount of fat. Gristle appears only in shin or chuck steak and any white streaks may be left on. Cuts with bone should be divided into slightly larger pieces.

Heat pan or casserole well before putting in the dripping or oil. Put in meat just to cover bottom of pan, and leave enough room to turn pieces comfortably. Fry on full heat for beef (not so fierce for veal or lamb) until meat is evenly browned (about $3\frac{1}{2}$ minutes). Turn each piece and brown for the same time on the other side. Do not fry for longer than 7 minutes.

Now take out meat, keep hot and add vegetables as specified in recipe. Lower heat and allow to colour. Pour off all excess fat but for 1-2 tablespoons. Add flour (about 1 dessertspoon — 1 tablespoon for $\frac{3}{4}$-1 pint stock); use slightly less if stock is jellied. Colour flour slowly for 2-3 minutes, scraping it gently from bottom of pan or casserole with a metal spoon.

Now add stock (1 pint for $1\frac{1}{2}$ lb solid meat). It is better to add two-thirds of the given quantity first, and bring it to the boil. Replace meat. Then add remainder of stock so that it comes just below level of meat. Add specified flavouring, cover pan or casserole tightly and cook as specified in the recipe.

If pre-cooking a stew ready for eating later on, transfer to a cold container so that it cools quickly; when reheating, bring to the boil before keeping warm (high temperature will kill any bacteria that may be present).

The best stewing cuts are:

Beef: chuck or shoulder steak (cut from the blade bone); clod; sticking; skirt.

Mutton or lamb: middle neck; double scrag or scrag; fillet end of leg.

Veal: breast; knuckle; cuts from the shoulder.

Rabbit: tame (Ostend) or wild rabbit in joints or whole.

When a cut contains a fair quantity of bone, as with neck or breast, allow a little more than for cuts that are solid meat.

Types of stew

Fricassée. This describes various stews of meat, poultry, fish or vegetables, usually made with a white stock. In France this term refers almost exclusively to a poultry dish in a white sauce.

Ragoût (brown). Pieces of meat, poultry or fish are lightly browned and then slowly cooked in stock to which vegetables are added.

Salmis. This is a type of ragoût, usually of game or poultry. The meat is first lightly roasted, then jointed and gently simmered for a short time in a rich, brown sauce.

Blanquette. This is a white ragoût of lamb, veal, chicken or rabbit, bound with egg yolks and cream, and sometimes garnished with small onions and mushrooms.

Navarin. This is the French word for a mutton or lamb stew made with root vegetables.

Certain vegetables are good stewed on their own, especially white ones such as onions, celery, artichokes and chicory.

Ragoût of beef

1½ lb chuck steak, or skirt
12 button onions
2 tablespoons dripping, or bacon
  fat
1 rounded dessertspoon plain flour
1 wineglass red wine
bouquet garni
1 clove of garlic (crushed with salt)
1 pint brown bone stock
salt and pepper
1 head of celery (trimmed)
½ oz butter
1 oz walnuts (shelled)
1 dessertspoon shredded orange
  rind

Method

Cut beef into 2-inch squares
and peel onions. Heat thick
casserole and put in fat. When
hot, lay in pieces of meat;
fry until brown, turning pieces
once. Take out meat, add onions
and fry slowly until beginning
to colour. Draw off heat, drain
so that only 1 tablespoon of fat
is left in the casserole. Stir in
flour, add red wine, meat,
bouquet garni and garlic. Barely
cover with stock, season, bring
slowly to the boil, cover and
simmer gently until tender
(1½–2 hours).

Meanwhile, cut the trimmed
head of celery into slices cross-
wise. Heat the butter in a
frying pan, put in walnuts and
celery and toss over the heat
with a pinch of salt, keeping
celery crisp. Then shred and
blanch orange rind in boiling
water until tender, drain and
rinse. Dish up ragoût, or leave
in casserole for serving, and
scatter celery mixture on the
top with the orange rind.

Paprika goulash

1½ lb chuck, or blade bone, steak
2 tablespoons dripping, or oil
8 oz onions (sliced)
1 tablespoon paprika pepper
1 tablespoon flour
1 dessertspoon tomato purée
  (canned, or in tube)
¾–1 pint stock
bouquet garni
1 clove of garlic (crushed)
salt and pepper
1 sweet pepper (red or green), or
  1 cap of canned pimiento
2 large tomatoes
4 tablespoons soured cream

Method

Cut meat into large squares,
brown quickly in pan of hot
dripping or oil and take out.
Lower heat and put in sliced
onions; after 3-4 minutes, add
paprika. Cook slowly for 1
minute, then add flour, tomato
purée and stock. Stir until
boiling, replace meat, add
bouquet garni, garlic and
seasoning. Cover and simmer
gently for 2 hours, or until
meat is very tender, on top of
stove or in the oven at 325°F
or Mark 3.

Blanch, peel and shred the
pepper or finely chop the pimiento; scald and peel the tomatoes, remove hard core and
seeds, then slice flesh. Now
add to goulash together with
the pepper (or pimiento). Bring
slowly to the boil and dish up.

Spoon over a little sour cream
and stir in gently.

Fricassée of rabbit

4–5 pieces of Ostend rabbit, or 1 wild rabbit (jointed)
white stock, or water (to cover meat)
2 onions (sliced)
bouquet garni
2 oz button mushrooms
½ oz butter

For sauce
1½ oz butter
3 tablespoons plain flour
¼ pint creamy milk

Method

Soak rabbit thoroughly in salted water, changing it from time to time. Blanch by putting into cold water, bringing to the boil, draining and refreshing. Trim away any pieces of skin with scissors and neaten the joints. Put rabbit into a shallow pan, barely cover with stock or water and add sliced onions.

For a more delicate flavour, blanch the onions first (by putting into cold water and bringing to the boil). Put in the bouquet garni, cover and simmer for 1-2 hours, or until very tender. Ostend rabbit takes less time than wild rabbit. Then drain off liquid, which should measure about ¾ pint.

Now make a roux in a saucepan with the butter and flour (see page 70), cook for about ½ minute, cool a little and strain on the liquid. Blend and stir until boiling. Boil gently until it is the consistency of thick cream; add the milk and continue cooking. At the same time, sauté the mushrooms in butter in another pan. Add these to the sauce and pour it over the rabbit. Turn the fricassée into a covered dish and leave in a warm oven for 5 minutes before serving. This allows the flavour of the sauce to penetrate the meat.

How to casserole

Casserole cooking is allied to pot roasting. The difference is that the ingredients are cooked in a liquid or sauce, and the meat or poultry is cut up or jointed before the final cooking — not left whole as in pot roasting. Other additions, such as mushrooms and tomatoes, are cooked with the main ingredients.

A casserole is cooked in the dish in which it is served, and as this was usually made of earthenware suited only to cooking in the oven, the food used not to be browned first. Today, there are many types of flameproof casseroles on the market so that meat or poultry can conveniently be browned on top of the stove before cooking.

The great advantage of casserole cooking is that once in the oven, very little or no last-minute attention to the dish is necessary.

Rabbit and bacon casserole

1 rabbit (jointed)
dash of vinegar
2 tablespoons dripping
1 small onion (finely chopped)
1 tablespoon flour
$\frac{3}{4}$–1 pint white stock
bouquet garni
1 rounded teaspoon tomato purée
1 clove of garlic (chopped)
salt and pepper
4 oz streaky bacon (in the piece)
12 pickling onions, or shallots

Method

Trim rabbit joints and soak over-night in salted water with a dash of vinegar. Drain and dry well.

Brown joints slowly in hot dripping in a thick casserole. Add chopped onion, sprinkle in flour. Turn joints over to coat them in mixture and fry for 1 minute. Then draw aside, add enough stock barely to cover, and herbs, purée and garlic. Season lightly, cover pan tightly and cook for 30 minutes in oven at 350°F or Mark 4. Meanwhile, cut bacon into short strips, blanch with pickling onions or shallots (put in cold water, bring to boil). Then drain and add to rabbit. Continue to cook for 1 hour or until all is tender. Remove bouquet garni, serve in casserole.

Chicken béarnais

1–2½ lb chicken
1–2 oz butter, or bacon fat
1 large onion
4 oz gammon rasher (in the piece)
6–8 baby carrots, quartered
1 wineglass white wine, or stock
salt and pepper
3 large tomatoes
2 cloves of garlic
2 tablespoons double cream (optional)
parsley (chopped) – to garnish

The Béarn province in the French Pyrénées is well known for its good food and local wines.

Method

Joint chicken (or ask butcher to do it); when jointing a whole bird for a casserole, put in the back for extra flavour, especially if you have to use water instead of stock. Fry joints slowly until golden-brown in the fat, then take out.

Slice onion thinly, cut gam-mon into squares, blanch both in cold water (bring to the boil and drain). Blanch carrots, lay them in bottom of casserole. Arrange chicken on top, together with onion and bacon. Moisten with wine, or stock, season lightly, cover and cook gently for 1 hour in oven at 350°F or Mark 4.

Skin and slice tomatoes, flick out seeds, add flesh to casserole with garlic crushed with salt. Cover, replace in oven. Continue to cook for 15 minutes or until chicken and carrots are tender. Take out the back of chicken before serving.

Finish, if wished, with the thick cream poured over top just before serving. Dust with chopped parsley.

How to pot roast

Pot roasting is one of the best and easiest ways of dealing with the cheaper cuts of meat that need slow cooking to prevent them from becoming dry and tasteless. Poultry is also excellent pot roasted, not only the older boiling fowls, but roasting birds and baby chickens too, because they keep all their flavour and succulence.

This method has the great advantage of requiring the minimum of attention once the meat is cooking. The only proviso is that you must have the right type of pot or casserole. This should be of thick iron, enamelled iron or aluminium with a close-fitting lid, deep and big enough to hold a joint or bird comfortably.

The procedure is simple: meat or bird is browned all over, root vegetables and a bouquet garni are added, but no liquid unless stipulated in the recipe. Even then it should not be more than one-eighth of a pint, ie. a small wineglass of stock or wine. A small quantity of seasoning is also added. Close the lid tightly and set on a low heat; if more convenient, put into a slow oven. Cooking time depends on the size of joint or bird.

Meat is served as for a roast, with vegetables cooked separately. If vegetables were cooked with the meat, they would have little flavour and would be overcooked. The flavour will be in the gravy; this is strained off, well skimmed of fat and may be diluted with a little stock. Once pot roasted, meat or chicken can be served in different ways, varied by sauces and garnishes.

Beef pot roast

2½ lb joint topside beef
1 tablespoon dripping
1 onion (stuck with a clove)
1 carrot (sliced)
bouquet garni
salt
pepper (ground from mill)
1 wineglass red wine, or stock
1 dessertspoon plain flour (for gravy)
little extra stock, or water, to taste

Method

Heat dripping in the pot. Put the meat in and brown well on all sides. Take out and pour off any surplus fat, leaving 1 tablespoon on the bottom. Replace meat and tuck the prepared vegetables down the sides with the herbs.

Pour over liquid and season very lightly. Lay a piece of buttered paper over the meat so that the cover fits tightly on top and there is no danger of the meat getting hard from contact with the lid while cooking. Set on low heat or, if preferred, in the oven at 325°F or Mark 3. Cook at least 2-3 hours or until the meat is tender, turning it over once or twice if cooking on the top of the stove.

Dish up the meat, skim off the fat, strain off the juice. Mix 1 dessertspoon of this fat with 1 dessertspoon flour. Add to the juice and dilute with a little extra stock or water to taste, and boil for about 5 minutes to cook the flour. This meat juice is concentrated.

Slice meat for serving, spoon over gravy. Garnish with the chosen vegetables or serve separately.

Fowl-in-the-pot

3½–4 lb boiling fowl
½–1 oz butter, or dripping
3 rashers of bacon (streaky)
1 onion (sliced)
1 carrot (sliced)
stick of celery (sliced)
bouquet garni
salt and pepper

For garnish
chipolata sausages and bacon rolls

Method

Brown the bird carefully all over in the pot with butter or dripping. Then take out, pour off all fat (there is a lot in a boiling fowl). Lay the bacon rashers on the bottom of the pot, set the bird on them and surround with the prepared vegetables. Add herbs and season lightly.

Cover with foil and put on the lid. Set on very low heat for 2½-3 hours, according to the size of the bird, or cook in a slow oven at 300°F or Mark 2. Avoid taking off the lid, particularly for the first 1½ hours. Pierce the thigh meat with a skewer to test for tenderness. Take out of pot and dish up with strained gravy as for the beef pot roast.

To make serving easier, the bird may be carved in the kitchen and dished up in a shallow casserole with a lid on. Spoon gravy over meat and, if you wish, garnish the dish with chipolata sausages and bacon rolls (rolled, skewered and then grilled).

How to Braise

Cheaper cuts of meat are often full of flavour but inclined to be tough, so braising is the ideal way of cooking them. The meat is tender and succulent and the rich, strong gravy it was cooked in is a bonus. For a good braise it's essential to use a very small quantity of liquid in a pot with a tight-fitting lid. The meat cooks in the steam from the liquid, thus keeping moist. Most of the cooking is done in the oven so that the braise has both top and bottom heat.

Choosing the right pan is important; it should be of enamelled iron, cast iron or thick aluminium and be deep enough for the joint to fit snugly into it. Glass, or any non-flameproof ovenware, however, is not suitable as part of the cooking is done on top of the stove.

Braising meat and game

Heat the pan and add 2 table-spoons of oil or dripping. When hot, put in the meat and brown well all over. Take out meat and put in a good plateful of sliced or diced vegetables (onion, carrot, a little turnip and celery). This is called a mirepoix.

Cover pan and cook gently (or sweat) for 5-7 minutes. This allows the juice to run from the vegetables and lets them absorb excess fat. Put back the meat on top of the mirepoix, together with a bouquet garni and a little seasoning.

Pour in liquid as required in the recipe. This should cover the bottom of the pan up to a level of 2-3 inches. Cover tightly and cook for 1-2 hours (according to the size of the joint) in a slow oven at 325°F or Mark 3.

Baste and turn the meat occasionally; it should be very tender when cooked. If you choose to braise a roasting joint, less time can be allowed (20 minutes per lb and 20 minutes over).

When meat is tender, remove it from pan and keep warm. Strain the gravy and skim surface well to take off any fat. A sauce can be added, depending on the recipe, or gravy can be thickened with kneaded butter or arrowroot. The vegetables cooked with the braise are now discarded as they will be over-cooked.

When braising a roasting joint, such as a leg of lamb, the vegetables can be served with the meat as the cooking time is not so long.

Watchpoint For a really successful braise it is essential to have a slightly jellied brown stock (see page 67). If the stock is not strong, a pig's foot (trotter) tucked in beside the joint gives a beautifully 'sticky'

texture to the finished sauce.

Braising fish
Braising is an excellent way of cooking whole fish, such as haddock or carp. The fish may first be stuffed with a herb mixture and then laid on the mirepoix of vegetables. Pour round a glass of cider, white wine or water, add salt and pepper and a bouquet garni. Cover pot tightly and braise as for meat.

Allow about 15-20 minutes per lb for large fish and about 20-25 minutes total cooking time for small fish. The fish is served with the juice lightly thickened with arrowroot, and sprinkled with chopped parsley.

Braising vegetables
Good braising vegetables are onions, celery, chicory, cabbage and lettuce. They are first blanched (for root vegetables, put into cold water and bring to the boil; for green vegetables, put into boiling water and re-boil before draining thoroughly). This blanching is done to remove any strong flavour and ensure thorough cooking.

Joints for braising

Beef	Aitchbone, topside, top rump, top rib, brisket.
Mutton or Lamb	Leg, shoulder (plain, or boned and stuffed), loin (boned and stuffed).
Veal	Cuts from leg and shoulder (plain, or boned and stuffed).

How to braise
continued

Arrowroot and cornflour

Both arrowroot and corn-flour are thickening agents.

Arrowroot is best used when making clear sauces or fruit syrups because it becomes clear once it has thickened. It is also used for thickening where the amount of liquid remaining in a meat dish is unknown until the end of cooking time (it can be difficult to judge how much juice or gravy will be left in a dish). The arrowroot should be slaked with a little cold liquid and then added to the residue which requires thickening.

As a rule, cornflour is used for blancmanges, custards and thick, white sauces for coating. The longer you cook it, the thicker it gets, whereas arrowroot jells on boiling and becomes thinner after boiling for 1 minute, not thicker. To prevent lumps forming, always mix corn-flour to a paste with a little cold water before adding to hot liquid.

Fricandeau

2½–3 lb fillet, or oyster, of veal
2 oz larding bacon
3–4 rashers of streaky fat bacon
2 large carrots (cut into rounds)
2 large onions (cut into rounds)
1 wineglass white wine
½–¾ pint jellied white stock
salt and pepper
bouquet garni

For spinach purée
2 lb spinach
1–2 tablespoons double cream, or white sauce

Method

Trim the meat, lard with bacon. Lay bacon rashers in the bottom of a braising pan. Place the vegetables on this, cover and cook gently for 5-7 minutes. Put in veal, add wine, ½ pint stock, seasoning and bouquet garni. Bring to the boil and braise for about 1-1½ hours in the oven at 325°F or Mark 3, basting frequently. Add extra stock if there's too much reduction.

Remove cooked meat, strain gravy and skim off fat. Return meat and gravy to the pan and cook on top of the stove on a brisk heat, basting well to glaze the meat a little. Remove meat; if necessary boil gravy rapidly to reduce and thicken.

To make spinach purée: boil spinach in salted water, drain, press well with a spoon to remove as much liquid as possible. Sieve, add cream or sauce.

Carve meat, serve on bed of spinach purée. Spoon over gravy.

To make a purée of sorrel and spinach, add a few handfuls of fresh sorrel with the spinach.

How to marinate

Marinating is a process of soaking meat, game or fish in a mixture of wine, oil, vegetables, herbs and spices. The object is to give flavour and, in the case of meat or game, to render it more tender as the presence of the oil in the marinade helps to soften the fibres. Most marinades, that is those for joints and which contain wine, vegetables, etc., are first boiled before use. A quick, uncooked marinade, however, may be used with foods such as steaks and fish fillets.

For a boiled marinade the ingredients are first brought to the boil and then left to get quite cold before being poured over the joint. As the amount of the marinade is small, the meat must be put into a bowl or deep dish, small enough for it to fit snugly. Turn the joint occasionally and see that the vegetables in the marinade sit on top to keep the joint moist. The marinade is then either added with the stock at the start of the cooking or strained into the liquid just before serving.

With a boiled marinade for beef or lamb, let meat stand in it for 24 hours, and for game up to 3 days. With an uncooked, quick marinade allow steak or fish to stand in the liquid 2-3 hours before cooking.

Marinade for beef

(for a joint of about $2\frac{1}{2}$ lb)

1 large onion
1 large carrot
1 stick of celery (optional)
1 large clove of garlic (peeled)
6–8 peppercorns
2 tablespoons olive oil
bouquet garni
2 wineglasses red wine (Burgundy or Burgundy-type, or any robust red wine)

Method

Cut the vegetables into thin slices, bruise the peeled clove of garlic but leave whole (chop garlic if a stronger flavour is liked). Put these into a pan with the other ingredients, cover and bring to the boil Simmer for 2 minutes, then pour off and leave until cold.

Quick marinade
(for grilled steaks, fish, and meat for a terrine)

1 dessertspoon finely chopped or sliced onion
2–3 tablespoons olive oil
1 teaspoon of lemon juice, or wine vinegar
black pepper (ground from mill)
2–3 tablespoons Madeira, or golden sherry (for steak marinade)

Method

Lay meat or fish on a dish and sprinkle over the ingredients. Give a good grinding of black pepper to finish. Leave at least 2 hours before cooking.

Marinade for game, venison and hare

Ingredients as for beef marinade, plus:

2 tablespoons red wine vinegar
2 parings of lemon rind
6 allspice, or juniper berries (crushed)

Method

Prepare as for beef marinade. Rich, dark meat such as venison calls for extra sharpness and seasoning, and spices can be altered to taste.

Hare is highly flavoured and excellent to eat. For jugged hare you don't have to marinate the meat before braising, but this soaking will improve the finished dish.

A hare is at its best when young (up to its second year). The male is called a buck and the female a doe. The French call a young leveret up to three months a *financier*, up to six months a *trois-quarts*, and at a year a *capucin* or *lièvre pit*.

See page 130 for instructions on how to prepare a hare.

Jugged hare

Legs and wings of hare, or 1 hare jointed (with the blood)
1 tablespoon dripping
2 onions (diced)
2 carrots (diced)
1 stick of celery (sliced)
bouquet garni
1½ pints white stock, or water
1 tablespoon redcurrant jelly, preferably home-made
1 small glass port wine
1 teaspoon arrowroot (to thicken), or kneaded butter

For forcemeat balls
1 oz butter
1 shallot, or small onion (finely chopped)
1 teacup fresh breadcrumbs
1 dessertspoon dried herbs
1 dessertspoon chopped parsley
salt and pepper
beaten egg, or milk (to bind)

For frying
seasoned flour
1 egg (beaten)
dried white breadcrumbs
deep fat bath

Method

Marinate hare overnight. Then drain and strain marinade. Braise the hare (see general instructions, page 124), then lift the pieces of cooked hare into a casserole for serving. Strain the gravy into a pan, skim off fat and add redcurrant jelly and the port.

Now make forcemeat balls: melt butter in a pan, add onion, cover and cook until soft but not coloured. Mix breadcrumbs, herbs and seasoning together in a basin, add the onion and enough beaten egg or milk to bind. Shape mixture into small balls, roll in seasoned flour then egg and crumb (see page 144). Set aside on a plate.

Boil gravy and reduce a little, if necessary, to give a good strong flavour. Draw aside and stir in the blood mixed with the arrowroot. Stir over heat until it has the consistency of cream but do not boil. Pour sauce over the hare and reheat in the oven for 5 minutes.

Heat fat bath; when at correct frying temperature (see page 150), lower in forcemeat on draining spoon and fry until golden-brown. Drain on absorbent paper. Then serve with the hare.

Watchpoint If the blood is not available, kneaded butter can be used to thicken the sauce. The blood binds the sauce together while the arrowroot helps to prevent it curdling.

Preparing a hare

The hind legs and wings (forelegs) of the hare are usually braised or jugged, while the back or saddle is kept for roasting. If the hare is not very large the whole may be jugged.

The hare should be jointed, the legs cut in two and the back into 3-4 pieces. With scissors trim away the rib cage and the flaps of skin that are attached to the pieces of back. Do not wash but wipe well. The joints can then be marinated which greatly improves the flavour and texture of the meat. If buying the whole hare rather than a few joints, ask for the blood as well. This is used to thicken the sauce.

If the hare is freshly killed it should be hung for 8-12 days according to the weather, head downwards, so that the blood can collect in the rib cage. Take care when skinning or jointing the hare not to break the membrane in the rib cage until you have a container ready to hold the blood. If marinating the hare, keep the blood in the refrigerator; 1-2 drops of vinegar added to it will prevent it from clotting.

How to grill

As a method of cooking, grilling has certain advantages; it is quick, straightforward and good for a meal which has to be on the table in a hurry; it is ideal for the diet-conscious because grills have little fat and almost no liquid. However, cuts have to be of the best quality, so a grill is not a cheap dish. On the following pages, you will find basic rules for grilling, together with recipes for grills, savoury butters and sauces.

Since a grill is a last-minute dish and one that should be served at once, it is not easy for the cook/hostess. Some grills such as cutlets, chops and kebabs can be kept hot for a short time in the grill pan with the juices, and heat turned low. Steaks, however, should be served at once. All grilling calls for a certain amount of attention, especially gammon steaks which tend to be dry unless brushed with melted butter or oil every 2-3 minutes.

The grill should be turned on at least 5-6 minutes before use to get the maximum heat. While it is heating leave grill pan underneath with grid set at right height. If food is getting overcooked when actually grilling, lower grid rather than grill heat.

Do not salt meat or fish before grilling; this causes juices to run, making food less succulent, but it may be peppered (ground from mill). Then brush meat with oil, turn over once or twice while grilling, keeping well brushed with oil (or as specified in individual recipe).

Buy the best cooking oil you can afford. Olive oil is the finest, but you can also use groundnut, or corn-based, oil instead. It is more economical to buy large tins or bottles. The given times for grilling are approximate, depending on the grill, thickness of food and whether or not it is to be pink inside or well done. A rule-of-thumb guide for steak is to press with your fingers: if it gives like a sponge, it is rare; if firmer and more resilient — medium rare; or firm with no resilience — well done.

How to 'dry' fry

If your grill is not a very efficient one or you have a solid fuel cooker, use the method known as dry frying. Take a thick, heavy frying pan — iron, ridged or enamelled iron, or cast aluminium. Set on full heat for several minutes, then put in 1 table-spoon of oil or dripping (free from gravy). When hot put in meat. Keep on full heat until well browned on one side, pressing the food well down with a palette knife; then turn and brown on the other side.

Time this process and lower heat if necessary to complete cooking. The time will vary, depending on what is being grilled and how well cooked it is to be (see chart overleaf).

Grills should be accompanied by savoury butters (see pages 137-138) served separately or in pats on top of steak, cutlets, etc. Grilled meats look best when served plainly garnished with a sprig of watercress and chip/jacket potatoes. A mixed green salad also goes well with a grill.

STEAK CUTS

Rump (1½ lb slice, 1 inch thick, serves 3-4)
This steak has incomparable flavour but to be tender must be
well hung. A guide to this is the colour, which should have a
purplish tinge with creamy-white fat. It improves if brushed
with oil 1-2 hours before grilling. During grilling time
brush once or twice with oil to prevent scorching.

Sirloin or entrecôte (¾-1 inch thick, serves 1)
This steak is cut from the top part of the sirloin.

Minute (½ inch thick, serves 1)
Thin slice of entrecôte. This steak should be cooked very rapidly and to
get it properly browned without over-cooking, dry fry rather than grill.

T-Bone (1½-2 inches thick, serves 2-3)
A whole slice cut from the sirloin with the bone.

Porterhouse (1½-2 inches thick, serves 1-2)
A slice cut from the wing rib, taken off the bone.

Fillet (1-1½ inches thick, serves 1)
The most expensive and possibly most tender of steaks.
There is a large demand for these slices cut across the fillet,
so they are in short supply. The fillet (averaging 6-7 lb) lies
under the sirloin and there is a comparatively small proportion
of fillet in relation to the weight of the rest of the animal. Dry fry or grill.

Tournedos (1-1½ inches thick, serves 1)
These are cut from the 'eye' of the fillet, ie. from centre after
it has been trimmed (fillet steaks include the side or edges,
ie. trimmings). A tournedos is very much a delicacy and may
be served plainly grilled or dry fried with a garnish as for a
fillet steak, or as a dish such as tournedos chasseur. The crisp
dry fat in which fillet is encased (kidney suet) is very special;
a small nut of this may be fried or grilled to top each tournedos.

Chateaubriand (3-4 inches thick, serves 2)
A thick cut taken from the heart of the fillet. This steak, once
grilled or dry fried, is sliced downwards for serving.

GRILLING TIMES   ACCOMPANIMENTS

Rare :	6-7 minutes	Maître d'hôtel or garlic butter,
Medium rare :	8-10 minutes	chip or jacket potatoes and
Well done :	14-16 minutes	fried onions. Vegetables : runner or French beans ; peas ; green salad.

Rare :	5 minutes	Maître d'hôtel or garlic butter,
Medium rare :	6-7 minutes	chip or jacket potatoes.
Well done :	9-10 minutes	Vegetables : chicory with butter ; green salad.

Rare :	$1-1\frac{1}{2}$ minutes	Maître d'hôtel or garlic butter,
Medium rare :	2-3 minutes	garnish with watercress ; chip potatoes and green salad.

Rare :	7-8 minutes	Maître d'hôtel or garlic butter,
Medium rare :	8-10 minutes	chip or jacket potatoes.

Rare :	7-8 minutes	Maître d'hôtel or garlic butter,
Medium rare :	8-10 minutes	chip or jacket potatoes.

Rare :	6 minutes	Béarnaise sauce or juices from the pan. Garnish with
Medium rare to well done :	7-8 minutes	mushrooms ; chip potatoes.

Rare :	6 minutes	Béarnaise sauce, or other sauces and vegetables
Medium rare to well done :	7-8 minutes	according to recipe.

Rare to medium rare :	16-20 minutes	Béarnaise sauce. For savoury butters, see pages 137-138.

Lamb

Cutlets

These are taken from the best end of neck and though cutlets may be bought ready-cut and trimmed, it is more economical to buy the neck and prepare them at home.

Ask the butcher to chine the neck for you, that is to saw the half backbone (chine bone) through so that the cutlets can be easily divided. He will also saw through the end bones to shorten them by about 2-3 inches. Cut away this 'flap' which can then be divided into 4-5 pieces and grilled with the cutlets. The chine bone is also detached and used for broth or gravy. A whole best end contains 6-7 cutlet bones with an average weight of $1\frac{1}{2}$-2 lb, depending on the size of the animal.

Cutlets must be plump, otherwise they curl when grilled or dry fried and become dry and tasteless. If the neck is medium size, allow 5 cutlets from a whole piece of best end; this gives a nut of meat $\frac{3}{4}$-1 inch thick.

Divide the neck into cutlets with a sharp knife, taking two bones if necessary. Cut out the second bone and any excess fat. Leave a rim of fat (about $\frac{1}{4}$ inch) round the meat and the small piece that lies just under it. Scrape the bone clean.

To be attractive, cutlets must be well trimmed; fat trimmings can be rendered down for use as dripping.

Brush with fat or oil and cook on grid or base of grilling pan for 7-8 minutes, turning once or twice and keeping well brushed with fat. The cutlets should be well browned with the fat crisp on the outside, and delicately pink when cut. Serve plain or with pats of savoury butter and sauté cucumber with spring onions or peas and baby carrots.

Noisettes

These are cutlets without the bone. Butchers will cut them for you, but you can prepare them at home. Take the best end unchined and start boning at the chine bone end. Use a small sharp knife and with short strokes cut down to, and along, the cutlet bones. Keep the knife well pressed on to the bones to avoid cutting into meat.

When the bone is out, season cut surface of the meat and roll up, starting at chine end. Trim off the end piece if there is more than enough to wrap once round the nut of meat. Tie securely at 1-$1\frac{1}{4}$ inch intervals with fine string, then cut between each tie. Grill as for lamb cutlets.

Chops

Loin chops are bought ready-cut and trimmed, and are 1-$1\frac{1}{2}$ inches thick.

Brush with oil and grill 8-9 minutes as for lamb cutlets. They should be well browned but slightly pink when cut. Serve with savoury butter. Best vegetables are runner beans; courgettes in butter; new or creamed potatoes.

Kebabs

The traditional shashlik, ie. skewer, dish consists of square chunks of meat, usually lamb, cut from the shoulder or leg and threaded on to long metal skewers, interspersed with slices of onion and bayleaves. But a mixture can be made from chipolata sausages, bacon rolls and pieces of lamb or fillet steak. Put these on a skewer, brush with melted butter and grill, turning skewer to cook chunks evenly. Dish up on boiled rice.

Kidneys

Lamb's kidneys are a classic ingredient of a mixed grill. To prepare, carefully peel off the hard fat which encases them (imported kidneys have this already removed). This suet rendered down, makes an excellent frying fat or dripping.

Skin kidneys by nicking the skin on the rounded side and drawing it back towards the core. Pull gently to get out as much of the core as possible before cutting away the skin. Split open on the rounded side and thread a skewer through to keep flat. Brush with melted butter, grill rounded side first and brush with melted butter from time to time throughout cooking. Allow 6-8 minutes grilling time according to size. Don't overcook or they become very leathery. Serve kidneys with maître d'hôtel or anchovy butter.

Mixed grill

For a mixed grill, the following ingredients for one person are a guide: 1 cutlet, 1 kidney, 1 sausage, 1 tomato, 2 mushrooms, 1 rasher of bacon, watercress and maître d'hôtel butter.

First prepare cutlets and kidneys as directed. Do not prick sausages as this makes them more likely to burst when cooking. Halve tomatoes and season cut surface. Peel the mushrooms

(preferably large, flat ones) and cut stalks level with caps. De-rind and flatten bacon.

Grill tomatoes, rounded side first, and turn after 3-4 minutes. Dust tops with caster sugar, put a knob of butter on each and grill for the same time. Grill mushrooms in the same way, putting a knob of butter on each side. Lift on to a plate and keep hot. Grill bacon, then the sausages, allowing 7-8 minutes, turning them once. Dish up with tomatoes and mushrooms. Keep hot. Grill the cutlets and add to the dish. Top with kidneys and maître d'hôtel butter, garnish dish with watercress.

Pork

Chops

Loin chops are really the only cut of pork suitable for grilling. Trim neatly, remove surplus fat and brush with melted butter. Heat grill well and cook chops thoroughly for 5-7 minutes on each side, brushing with butter.

Garnish with watercress and serve with an apple or barbecue sauce, sauté potatoes and salad.

Gammon steaks

These are $\frac{1}{2}$-inch slices from the gammon of bacon which may be smoked or green, ie. un-smoked. The latter is milder in flavour. Cut away the rind and brush well with melted butter while grilling. Set the grid lower in the grill pan than for other meats. Allow about 7-8 minutes grilling time.

Garnish with fried pineapple slices. Serve with spinach, or runner or French beans, or peas and chip or sauté potatoes.

How to grill fish

Grilling is a good and attractive way of cooking small whole fish (round or flat), particularly the rich and oily variety such as herring and mackerel. The intense heat crisps the skin making the fish especially appetising. Also excellent as straightforward grills are sole and halibut, turbot and salmon steaks.

Like meat, fish should not be salted before grilling but served with various savoury butters, such as maître d'hôtel, anchovy, or orange, which give all the seasoning necessary; water-cress makes a good garnish.

Unlike oily fish, white fish needs to be well brushed both before and during the cooking, with ordinary melted (or for a better colour — clarified) butter.

When grilling round fish score, ie. make a diagonal cut to slit the skin, in 2-3 places to allow the heat to penetrate more easily and so shorten the cooking time. It is not necessary to do this scoring with flat fish unless they are very large.

Grilling times depend on the thickness of the fish, not on the weight.

The tails of these grilled mackerel have been vandyked — cut in an acute V-shape to accentuate the lines

Clarified butter

As this is an extravagant grilling or frying medium, it is best used for special occasions. For example, from 8 oz butter you only get about 6 oz clarified butter, but the end certainly justifies the means as the colour and taste of the food after cooking are quite excellent. The moisture and salt having been removed, the butter is less apt to burn when heated.

To clarify butter: take 8 oz or more of butter at a time (as it will keep when clarified), cut it up and put into a thick saucepan. Melt over slow heat and once melted continue to cook until it is foaming well. Skim well, strain through a muslin into a basin and leave to settle, then pour into another basin, leaving sediment behind.

The butter will then form a solid cake which can be used at once or melted down to pour into pots which should be covered before storing in the larder or refrigerator.

Noisette butter

1–2 oz butter
juice of ½ lemon

Method

Melt the butter in a pan and, when brown, add the lemon juice. Use while still foaming.

Savoury accompaniments

When these mixtures are made, pat into balls with butter 'hands' (wooden shaping boards), or spread out ¼-½-inch thick on greaseproof paper and chill. Then cut into small round or square pats before using. The quantities given are enough for 4 people.

Orange butter

2 oz unsalted butter
grated rind of ½ orange and 1 teaspoon juice
1 teaspoon tomato purée
salt and pepper

Method

Soften the butter on a plate with a palette knife, and then add other ingredients, seasoning to taste.

Serve chilled, in pats, with lamb cutlets, steaks and fish.

Maître d'hôtel butter

2 oz unsalted butter
1 dessertspoon chopped parsley
few drops of lemon juice
salt and pepper

Method

Soften the butter on a plate with a palette knife, then add parsley, lemon juice and seasoning to taste.

Serve chilled, in pats, with steaks, mixed grills and fish.

Savoury accompaniments

Anchovy butter

2 oz unsalted butter
4 anchovy fillets (soaked in milk to remove excess salt)
black pepper (ground from mill)
anchovy essence

Method

Soften the butter on a plate with a palette knife and then crush or pound the anchovies, adding these to the butter with ground pepper and enough essence to strengthen the flavour and give a delicate pink colour.

Serve with mutton, chops or cutlets, and fish.

Chutney, garlic, mustard or tomato butters

Other savoury butters are made in the same way using 2 oz unsalted butter with either pounded chutney, crushed garlic, 1 dessertspoon French mustard, or tomato purée.

Parsley butter

$\frac{1}{2}$ oz butter
1 teaspoon chopped parsley
dash of Worcestershire sauce, or squeeze of lemon juice

Method

Melt the butter in a pan and, when light and brown, add the chopped parsley and Worcestershire sauce or lemon juice. Blend together and then pour sauce over the meat.

Barbecue sauce

1 teaspoon flour
$\frac{1}{3}$ pint potato stock (water in which potatoes have been cooked)
1 tablespoon soy sauce
dash of Worcestershire sauce
salt and pepper.
2 tomatoes

Method

Skim off the fat from the grill pan, leaving about 1 dessert-spoon and any sediment. Stir in flour and cook very gently for 2-3 minutes. Draw aside and blend in potato stock, sauces and seasoning, then return to heat and stir until boiling. To skin the tomatoes: place them in a bowl, scald by pouring boiling water over them, count 12, then pour off the hot water and replace it with cold. The skin then comes off easily. Cut the flesh into shreds and add to the mixture. Simmer for 1 minute.

This sauce goes well with lamb kebabs or pork chops.

How to sauté

Sautéing is advanced work and is an important method of cooking, calling for care and a certain amount of judgment. This comes with practice. Meat, poultry and game are used for a sauté and must be young, tender and of best quality. A sauté is a quick dish to make and good for entertaining as it can be kept waiting without spoiling.

To sauté, fry lightly pieces of meat to seal in juices. Add a small quantity of strong stock, with or without wine. It should come barely level with meat or joints in pan and may at this point be lightly thickened.

When cooking is completed the sauce should be rich and concentrated with just enough to allow 2-3 tablespoons per person. To achieve this, a sauté pan (similar to a large deep frying pan but with straight sides and a lid) should be used. The wide base allows room for browning and for quick reduction of sauce. The lid helps to slow up this reduction, if necessary, and ensures the cooking of the meat. If you haven't a proper sauté pan, use your deepest frying pan with a pan lid or plate as a cover.

When the meat is arranged in the serving dish, you must use your own judgment as to whether the sauce should be further reduced to strengthen the flavour and thicken it a little more.

Watchpoint Care must be taken not to over-reduce, as this will give a harsh taste. If the flavour is right but the sauce is too thin, thicken with a tiny quantity of arrowroot mixed with a little cold water.

In more advanced recipes a previously made sauce is added towards end of cooking, the sauté taking its name from the sauce or any other ingredient or garnish.

To sauté is also a term used to describe cooking briskly in a small quantity of butter and/or oil and is particularly suitable for vegetables. Freshly boiled potatoes are delicious sautéd in butter until crisp and golden-brown in appearance, with a soft and buttery taste. Cold cooked leftover potatoes, while making a very good 'pan fry', are not the same thing.

Vegetables which can be sautéd raw, with a lid on the pan, include jerusalem artichokes, chicory, marrow, celery and leeks. They should be thickly sliced and cooked in butter with little or no liquid. They do not colour, but retain all their flavour and cook comparatively quickly in 7-10 minutes.

Sauté of chicken with red wine (mâconnaise)

2½–3 lb roasting chicken
1 tablespoon oil
1 oz butter
1 shallot (finely chopped)
2 wineglasses red wine (Burgundy)
½ pint demi-glace sauce (see page 78)

For croûtes
4 slices of a French roll
oil and butter (for frying)

Method

Joint chicken (or ask butcher to do it). Heat oil in a sauté pan, drop in butter and when foaming put in the joints, skin side down, in the following order:

First, the two legs and thighs which, being the thickest joints, need the longest cooking.

When these are beginning to brown, put in two wing joints, then whole breast (watch this tender joint carefully, turning when brown on one side, then remove from pan).

When remaining joints are golden-brown, turn them over, put in breast and shallot, cook gently for 2-3 minutes. Pour in wine, set alight to drive off alcohol and leave to simmer very gently for 10-15 minutes.

Fry the croûtes for garnish.

Pour the prepared demi-glace sauce on to chicken and simmer, uncovered, for about 2-3 minutes. Take up chicken, trim joints and then arrange on a hot serving dish. Spoon over sauce and garnish with croûtes.

Veal scaloppine à la crème

3–4 veal escalopes
1 oz butter
1 small onion (finely chopped)
1 small glass sherry
1 dessertspoon plain flour
$\frac{1}{4}$ pint veal bone stock
2 oz button mushrooms (sliced thinly)
salt and pepper
2 tablespoons double cream

Method

Cut escalopes (thin pieces of meat cut from leg or fillet) in half to form scaloppine (small escalopes). Heat a sauté pan, drop in the butter and, while still foaming, put in the pieces of veal. Cook briskly for 3-4 minutes, turning once, remove from the pan, add chopped onion and cook for 1-2 minutes; then pour on sherry.

Boil sherry to reduce a little, then draw aside. Stir in flour and stock, bring to the boil, add mushrooms and veal, and season. Cover the pan and simmer meat gently for 8-10 minutes. Taste for seasoning, add the cream and reheat without boiling.

Pork fillet sauté normande

$1\frac{1}{2}$ lb pork fillet/tenderloin
1 oz butter
1 medium-size onion (finely sliced)
1 dessert apple
1 tablespoon plain flour
1 wineglass dry cider
$\frac{1}{4}$ pint brown stock
salt and pepper
2 tablespoons double cream

Method

Brown pork fillet on all sides in the butter, remove from the pan, add the onion and cook for 2-3 minutes. Peel, core and slice the apple, add to the pan and continue cooking until both onion and apple are golden-brown. Stir in the flour, cider and stock and bring to the boil. Put the fillet back in the pan, season, cover the pan and simmer gently for 45-50 minutes until meat is tender. This can be done on top of the stove or in the oven at 350°F or Mark 4.

Remove the meat from the sauce, cut in slanting, $1\frac{1}{2}$-inch slices and place on a hot serving dish. Strain the sauce, reheat and then stir in the cream. Taste for seasoning and spoon over the meat.

Dishes **à la normande** are usually braised fish coated with a cream sauce (normande), but when referring to small cuts of meat or chicken the sauce includes some cider, and sometimes Calvados (the strong eau-de-vie liqueur made from apples).

The most famous eau-de-vie from apples originated in that part of Normandy known as Calvados (named after the Spanish Armada ship which was wrecked on nearby cliffs in 1588). Districts around Calvados are now allowed to use the name for their eau-de-vie.

How to fry

After roasting, frying is perhaps the next most important cooking process, and the advantages are that it is quick and simple to do.

There are two ways of frying, either in shallow or deep fat. Both methods cover a wide range of basic foods — meat, fish and made-up dishes too, such as fish cakes. It is important also to know how to prepare food for frying, so overleaf you will learn what coatings to use, with step-by-step photographs on how to egg and crumb, and how to make fritter batters.

Properly fried food should look appetising and taste light, leaving you wanting more.

Shallow fat frying

This is the most commonly used method and, as the name implies, it is done in a frying pan, in any of these fats : butter ; oil ; a mixture of butter and oil ; dripping ; lard or one of the commercially prepared fats.

Small whole fish, fillets of fish and fish cakes are suited to shallow fat frying. For the best taste and effect use butter, otherwise oil or dripping (do not use the latter with fish in an egg and crumb coating because dripping would over-brown the egg).

The amount of fat in the pan is important ; it should come half way up the fish so that the sides are completely browned.

Turn the fish once only and cook on moderate to brisk heat.

The same pan can be used for all types of food fried in shallow fat, any fat left over being strained off and used again, but fish fat should be kept only for fish frying.

Whole fish need only to be rolled in seasoned flour or oatmeal just before frying. Sole or plaice fillets may be rolled in seasoned flour and then fried in butter, or dipped in beaten egg after being rolled in seasoned flour, then fried until golden-brown.

Deep fat frying

This method is quicker than shallow fat frying as food is immersed completely. Therefore the fish needs a coating to protect it from the great heat of the fat.

When cool, strain used fat through muslin into a bowl, cover when it is quite cold, and store in a cool place until needed again.

Choose a deep, heavy gauge pan (fat bath or deep fryer) which covers the source of heat, complete with a wire basket to fit. Or buy a separate folding wire basket for fitting into any saucepan (which must, however, be of reasonably heavy gauge because fat is heated to high temperatures in deep fat frying). This separate basket is useful because its flexibility means it can also be used in an ordinary frying pan for cooking small foods such as croûtons.

When frying fish coated in soft batter mixture, you may find it easier to fry them in a fat bath without using a wire basket since batter tends to stick to the basket.

Suitable fats to use are : vegetable or nut oil ; lard ; clarified dripping or commercially prepared fat, but it is better not to mix these. Olive oil and margarine are not suitable for deep frying. The pan should not be more than one-third full of fat or oil.

Melt the fat, or put the oil, over moderate heat, then increase heat until right cooking temperature is reached (350-375°F). Oil must never be heated above 375°F and for sunflower oil, and some commercially prepared fats (eg. Spry, Cookeen), 360°F is the highest recommended temperature. It is important to remember that oil does not 'haze,' as solid fats do, until heated to a much higher temperature than is required — or is safe — for frying.

The fat or oil should never be below 340°F, as it is essential that the surface of the food is sealed immediately. This means that it does not absorb the fat, and is more digestible.

The best way of testing temperature is with a frying thermometer. Before using, it should be stood in a pan of hot water then carefully dried before putting into the fat bath. The hot water warms the glass so that it does not break when plunged into the hot fat.

If you have no thermometer, drop in a small piece of food (eg. a chip). If the fat or oil is at the right temperature, the food will rise immediately to the top and bubbles appear round it. Alternatively drop in a cube of day-old bread, which should turn golden-brown in 20 seconds at 375°F; 60 seconds at 360°F.

How to fry fish

For fish such as fillets of sole, or plaice, or small whole sole, an egg and breadcrumb coating is best.

Fish, such as haddock or whiting, which crumble more easily, are best fried in batter.

Most fried fish should be garnished with sprays of fried parsley and a savoury butter such as maître d'hôtel or anchovy, which should be served separately.

Watchpoint Great care should be taken when handling a deep fat bath or fryer. When fat is heating, make sure that the handle of the fat bath or fryer is pushed to one side so that there is no danger of it being caught or knocked over.

Fat is inflammable; if any is spilt, wipe it up at once. Keep the outside of the fat bath clean so that there is no chance of any fat catching alight, which can easily happen if it is overheated.

If fat does catch fire, smother it with a cloth — do not splash water on it or attempt to move the blazing pan. If you have to leave the kitchen at any time while cooking with fat, turn off the heat under the pan.

Coating skinned fillets of sole with seasoned flour for shallow frying

Coatings

There are three types of coatings: seasoned flour with beaten egg and dry white breadcrumbs (for fillets of fish, cutlets and croquettes, etc.); fritter batter (for fillets of fish, sweet and savoury fritters) and pastry.

To get a crisp, golden coating, dry white crumbs are essential, and a jar of these should be kept ready for use in the kitchen.

To make dry white crumbs: take a large loaf (the best type to use is a sandwich loaf) at least two days old. Cut off the crust and keep to one side. Break up bread into crumbs either by rubbing through a wire sieve or a Mouli sieve, or by working in an electric blender.

Spread crumbs on to a sheet of paper laid on a baking tin and cover with another sheet of paper to keep off any dust. Leave to dry in a warm place — the plate rack, or warming drawer, or the top of the oven, or even the airing cupboard, is ideal. The crumbs may take a day or two to dry thoroughly, and they must be crisp before storing in a jar. To make them uniformly fine, sift them through a wire bowl strainer.

To make browned crumbs: bake the crust in a slow oven until golden-brown, then crush or grind through a mincer. Sift and store as for white crumbs. These browned ones are known as raspings and are used for any dish that is coated with a sauce and browned in the oven.

Egging and crumbing

To make egging and crumbing easy, it is best to follow a certain technique. Whether frying fish or shaping a mixture, the first coating should always be of flour, lightly seasoned with a pinch of salt and half as much pepper.

Start with a board or plate well sprinkled with seasoned flour on the one side, have the beaten egg on a plate in the centre, and the white crumbs on a large piece of paper on the other side. You can then work from left to right, or vice versa, finally placing the coated food on to a large dish.

If using a mixture, first divide this into even-size portions, then shape on the floured board or plate (preferably with palette knives or round-bladed knives to avoid touching with your fingers). With the knives, lift the shaped mixture into the beaten egg (brushing evenly) and on to the paper of crumbs, still not touching with your fingers. Lift each corner of the paper, tipping mixture from side to side, and when well covered, press on the crumbs with a knife. Then lift off on to the large dish already sprinkled with crumbs. The croquettes — the name given to this type of crumbed mixture — are then ready for frying.

In the case of fillets of fish, these must be absolutely dry, so make sure that after washing they are thoroughly dried in absorbent paper or a cloth kept specially for this prupose.

Roll fillets in the seasoned flour and shake gently to remove any surplus. Then draw them through the beaten egg, first on one side, then the other, and gently run down the whole length of the fillet with your finger and thumb to wipe off any surplus egg. Turn on to the paper of crumbs, tip fillets from side to side to cover thoroughly and press on the crumbs with a palette knife until well coated. Lift off on to a dish or rack. When convenient, egging and crumbing may be done quite a time ahead.

1 *Divide mixture into even-size portions, shape on floured board*
2 *Lift the shaped mixtures with palette knives into beaten egg*

3 *Brush shapes evenly and then turn with the palette knives*
4 *After tipping in the paper of crumbs, press on with knives*

Fritter batters

There are two types of fritter batter; the quantities given for both types here are sufficient for fruit fritters for 4 people, but large portions of fish need at least half again as much batter mixture.

Fritters are called beignets in French, and the word is believed to come from the Celtic for 'swelling'.

Soufflé fritters, sometimes known as 'nun's sighs', are made from choux pastry, and after frying are rolled in caster sugar for serving with a sweet jam sauce, or with grated Parmesan cheese for savoury tastes.

Kromeski is the name given to small pieces of cooked, creamed chicken, veal or game mixture which are wrapped in thin bacon rashers before dipping in batter and frying.

Almost anything can be turned into a fritter, from cardoons (edible thistles) and chard (a white sea kale beet) to brains, tongue and truffles, oysters, rice and semolina, crystallised fruit, and even acacia blossoms or violets. But the most common choice is raw fruit, usually apples and bananas.

Fritter batter 1

4 tablespoons plain flour
pinch of salt
2 egg yolks
1 tablespoon melted butter, or oil
¼ pint milk
1 egg white

Method

Sift flour with salt into a bowl, make a well in centre of flour, add egg yolks, melted butter, or oil, and mix with milk to a smooth batter; beat thoroughly. Stand in a cool place for 30 minutes. Just before frying, whisk egg white stiffly, fold into batter. Fry in deep fat or up to ½-inch depth for shallow frying.

Fritter batter 2

5 oz plain flour
pinch of salt
small piece of fresh yeast about size
    of a nut, or 1 teaspoon dried yeast
1 teacup warm water
1 tablespoon oil
1 egg white (optional)

This deep-fry batter is slightly crisper than the first type.

Method

Sift flour and salt into a warm basin. Mix yeast in about half the warm water, stir into flour with oil. Add rest of water to make consistency of thick cream. Beat well and cover. Leave in a warm place for 15-20 minutes. By then mixture should be well risen. If using egg white, whisk stiffly and fold into batter just before frying.

Fish in batter

When frying fish in fritter batter, choose the second batter recipe and double the quantity for ease in working. For white fish such as haddock or cod fillet, allow $1\frac{1}{4}$-$1\frac{1}{2}$ lb for 4 people, skin and cut into 4-oz portions. Sprinkle lightly with salt and lemon juice, and leave for 30 minutes. Drain off any liquid, dry well and roll in seasoned flour.

Have batter ready in a bowl before heating fat. When fat is smoking hot, drop a piece of the fish into the batter bowl, turn to coat thoroughly, then lift out with a draining spoon and slide carefully into the fat bath. Fry about three pieces at a time, allowing plenty of room to turn them. When well browned and crisp, lift out and drain well on absorbent paper. Take out any scraps of batter before frying the next batch.

Fish cakes

1lb fresh haddock, or cod fillet, or
   12 oz cooked fish

little salt ⎫
butter   ⎬ if using fresh fish
lemon juice ⎭   only

3–4 medium-size potatoes
1 tablespoon butter
1 egg
salt and pepper
1 dessertspoon chopped parsley

For frying

seasoned flour
beaten egg
dry white breadcrumbs

This is a good way of using up leftovers. Make with white fish, fresh or canned salmon. The proportion of fish when cooked, skinned and flaked, should be equal that of potato. However, the fish can be more in quantity but never less.

Method

With fresh fish, wash and dry well, sprinkle with a little salt and if time allows, let it stand for 15-20 minutes. Tip off liquid, place fish in buttered, flame-proof dish, with a little lemon juice, cover with buttered paper and cook for 15–20 minutes in the oven at 350°F or Mark 4. Flake fish, remove skin and bones.

Now work prepared fish in a bowl to break up the fibres (if fish is inclined to be wet, eg. cold or canned salmon, this working of fish will thicken the consistency).

Boil potatoes, drain, dry and mash well. Beat in the butter, egg and fish; season well and add parsley. Put out in tablespoons on to a seasoned, floured board. Shape into cakes, brush with beaten egg, roll in (and press on) the crumbs. Fry, in either deep or shallow fat, when fat should be over $\frac{1}{2}$-inch deep in pan. Lift in the fish cakes when the fat is at the right temperature (350-375°F) and after browning on one side turn carefully. Drain when a good colour and serve hot with a tomato sauce or ketchup.

Fried fillets of sole or plaice

As a main course, allow 2 fillets per person from a fish weighing about $1\frac{1}{4}$ lb (skinned on both sides). Wash the fillets, dry thoroughly and roll in seasoned flour, beaten egg and white crumbs.

When ready to fry, heat the fat bath and place the basket in it. When the correct temperature is reached (refer to the temperature guide overleaf), take up fillets and holding each end between a finger and thumb, twist them. (This is done to avoid sogginess when deep fat frying. It reduces the flat surface which would normally come in too much contact with the serving dish and the other fillets. The resulting fillets also look more attractive.)

Lower the twisted fillets to the surface of the fat and gently let go; put in about three at a time. When fillets are a deep golden-brown, lift out basket and stand it on a plate or tray. Leave for 1-2 minutes before lifting out fillets on to a hot dish. Scatter over fried parsley and serve pats of maître d'hôtel butter separately.

Lower twisted fillet to fat surface and let go gently to avoid splashing

Chip potatoes (French fried)

$1\frac{1}{2}$ lb even-size potatoes (weighed
  when peeled)
deep fat, or at least 1-inch depth
  of fat in frying pan

Method

Prepare potatoes 1 hour before
needed. Square off ends and
sides of potatoes, cut in $\frac{1}{2}$-inch
thick slices, then into thick
fingers. Soak in cold water for
30 minutes, then drain. Wrap
in absorbent paper or cloth and
leave for 20-30 minutes. Heat
fat, dip in basket; when fat
reaches right temperature (see
chart overleaf), gently lower
into fat. If you do not have a
thermometer, drop in a finger
of potato; if this rises to surface
at once and fat starts to bubble
gently, fat is ready. Fry gently
until potatoes are just soft
but not coloured. Lift out and
drain, still in basket, on a plate.
Chips can be left like this for a
little while before the final
frying. Reheat fat to frying
temperature; carefully lower in
basket, fry chips to a deep
golden-brown. Drain well on
absorbent paper, turn into a
hot dish for serving and sprinkle
with salt. Potatoes double-fried
in this way are crisply tender on
the outside and evenly browned.
When cooking fish and chips,
fry potatoes first so that there is
no chance of crumb coating
from fish spoiling the fat for
the potatoes.

Temperature guide to frying

Uncooked doughs — fried on a rising temperature, eg. pirozhki, choux pastry	325°F-375°F
Fish fillets and cooked mixtures, eg. croquettes, fish cakes	350°F-375°F
Meat	350°F-375°F
Chips, game chips and whitebait — first frying — second frying	 350°F 360°F-375°F
Fritters — sweet and savoury	350°F-375°F

Fried parsley

Choose 6-7 sprays of fresh parsley. Wash and dry well. Once food is fried and taken out, put the individual parsley sprigs into the basket.

To avoid fat spluttering, turn off heat, wait until any blue haze has disappeared, then gently lower basket into the fat and fry for 1-2 minutes when parsley will be crisp and bright green. Drain on absorbent paper.

Fish

Types of fish

COD

Cod can weigh up to 80 lb and grow to about 4 feet. Known in France as *cabillaud* or *morue* (salt cod).

PLAICE

Plaice. Eat when really fresh. Freshness indicated by brightness of red spots on topside. In French, *plie.*

HADDOCK

Haddock is often split open and smoked. In French it is called *aiglefin,* and also *morue noire* (black cod).

SOLE

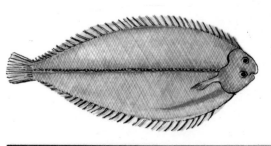

Sole. The colour of sole varies depending on depth of water in which it is fished. Same name in France.

HALIBUT

Halibut ranges from 2 lb-400 lb and up to 10 feet long! 'Chicken' halibut (2-5 lb) are thought best. In French, *flétan*.

SKATE

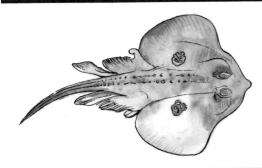

Skate. Only wings are usually eaten. Don't eat when very fresh as flesh is too tough. Known in France as *raie*.

Cleaning fish

To clean a round fish, slit skin below head, along belly to vent. Scrape out gut and throw away. Remove head, if wished. Wash fish under a running cold tap

To skin a round fish, lift tail end and slip knife in between flesh and skin. Hold tail firmly, saw flesh away from skin; keep knife at an angle to the board

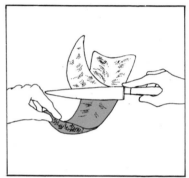

To skin a flat fish, cut fins off first. Then starting at head end, slip thumb about 1 inch under black skin at cut where fish was cleaned

Run thumb round fish, keeping it under the skin. Then grasp tail end firmly and rip skin off. Repeat this on other side of the fish

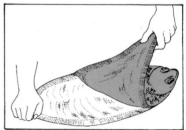

Filleting fish

To fillet a round fish, take a sharp knife and cut down back with knife blade on top of the backbone. Lift off the top fillet

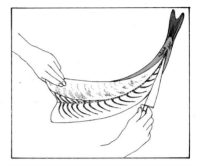

To remove other fillet, slip knife under backbone at head. Keep close to bone, work down to tail with short strokes

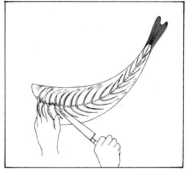

To fillet a flat fish, run knife down backbone; with short, sharp strokes, keep knife on bone and work from head outwards down to tail

To remove other fillet on same side, turn fish round. Start from tail end and take off fillet in same way. Repeat on the other side

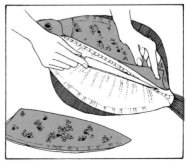

Ways of cooking white fish

Apart from grilling and frying, the most common method of cooking fish is known as boiling (really an incorrect term here for poaching), usually done on top of the stove. This is one of the best ways to cook fish simply, whole or in steaks, and a good contrasting sauce should accompany the fish. Poaching is cooking in a small quantity of liquid in the oven, or on top of the stove, and the resulting juices can then be turned into a coating sauce. All poached fish should be transferred to a clean serving dish before coating with a sauce. Any fish for cooking in this way, whether whole or as a large steak, should be done in a special stock, called court bouillon, rather than water. This is simple to prepare and once the fish has been cooked in it, the liquid should be strained off and used again for poaching or as liquid for a sauce (see recipe for poached cod on the next page). Cooking fish au gratin, a less well known method, is where small whole fish (fillets or steaks) are cooked in the oven in a thick, well-seasoned sauce and finished with a topping of browned crumbs, melted butter and sometimes cheese.

Soused herrings

6 herrings plus 2 extra for second
  helpings
salt and pepper
1 tablespoon pickling spice
1 bayleaf
1 onion (thinly sliced)
¾ pint vinegar and water (in equal
  proportions)

Method

Have herrings split and boned. Season cut surface and roll up from head to tail. Pack them in a deep dish or casserole. Set oven at 325°F or Mark 3.

Put pickling spice and bay-leaf into a pan with onion, vinegar and water. Add salt and bring to the boil. Cool, then pour over the herrings. The liquid should just cover them. Cook in the pre-set oven for about 1 hour. Serve the herrings cold.

Pickling spice is a selection of whole spices (peppercorns, allspice and mace, etc.) and is a convenient way of buying spices if you do not use them frequently. If not using pickling spice for soused herrings, you will need 6 peppercorns, 2 blades of mace, 2 allspice berries and 1 clove. For a milder flavoured souse, add 1 tablespoon brown sugar to the vinegar and water. White wine can replace vinegar if preferred.

Poached cod with egg or oyster sauce

2 lb steak of cod (or turbot, or halibut)

¾ pint egg, or oyster, sauce

For court bouillon
2 pints water
1 large carrot (sliced)
1 onion (sliced)
bouquet garni
6 peppercorns
2 tablespoons vinegar, or juice of ½ lemon

Egg or oyster sauce can also be used for turbot or halibut, although the traditional sauce for them is a shrimp or lobster one.

Method

Put ingredients for court bouillon in a pan, salt lightly, cover and simmer for 8-10 minutes; then leave to cool.

Tie fish in a piece of muslin, put in pan, cover and bring slowly to boil. Lower heat and barely simmer for 35-40 minutes. Take up and drain for 2-3 minutes before unwrapping muslin. Dish up on a hot dish and serve at once with your chosen sauce.

Egg sauce

This is a béchamel or white sauce, with the addition of chopped, hard-boiled egg.

Put ¾ pint milk with 1 bayleaf, slice of onion, blade of mace and 6 peppercorns into a pan. Infuse by covering and bringing slowly to scalding point. Pour off into a jug and cool slightly. Wipe out pan, melt 1 oz butter, gently stir in 1 rounded tablespoon plain flour off the heat, then strain on milk mixture about a third at a time. Season with salt and pepper. Blend well, then stir continually over heat until boiling. Boil for 1-2 minutes. Taste for seasoning then stir in 2 coarsely chopped hard-boiled eggs.

Oyster, shrimp or **lobster** sauce is made in the same way, but the fish is added in place of egg. A small tin of any of these shellfish is sufficient for the above amount of sauce.

Index